REAL-LIFE CHRISTIANITY

Jesus called people to follow him.

What does that mean in practice? *Real-life Christianity* gives very down-to-earth guidelines. It makes the link between Jesus' teaching and life today.

REAL-LIFE CHRISTIANITY

Andrew Knowles

A LION MANUAL

Text copyright © 1984 Andrew Knowles
This edition copyright © 1995 Lion Publishing

The author asserts the moral right
to be identified as the author of this work

Published by
Lion Publishing plc
Sandy Lane West, Oxford, England
ISBN 0 7459 2650 9
Albatross Books Pty Ltd
PO Box 320, Sutherland, NSW 2232, Australia
ISBN 0 7324 1217 X

A catalogue record for this book is available
from the British Library

Printed and bound in Malaysia

CONTENTS

Following Jesus   7

If we want to live Christian lives ourselves, we need to know how Jesus lived. What was he like? What did he teach? How did he relate to people?

We Have Lift-off!   25

Where do we get the strength to follow Jesus? Christianity is not just trying to imitate Christ. The good news is that he gives us his own power and love.

Where Now?   37

The foundation of a Christian life is very personal. Prayer, worship, Bible study, are the hidden heart of it, Christian living is the outcome.

Working It Out   56

Unless Christianity makes a down-to-earth difference, it is nothing. We must learn to follow Jesus in the everyday realities of life: home, sex, money, work . . .

Wider Still and Wider   82

Christian faith reaches beyond our backyard. We have to learn to apply Jesus' teaching to the great issues of the day, such as race, poverty, conservation.

FOLLOWING JESUS

What kind of person was Jesus?
What kind of life did he lead?

If we are to follow him today, we must take a
fresh look at his life on earth. We must follow in
his footsteps. Walk in his shoes.

A REAL LIFE

Jesus of Nazareth was no stained-glass window figure. He got breathtakingly involved with life on earth. Life as it really was and is for many millions of people.

The Son of God was born into a poor family in an occupied country. Not only were they far from home at the time, but they were also far from the medical security of today's hospitals and the comfortable trappings of the babywear chain store.

As Jesus grew up, he had no private schooling or college education. Indeed, the only advantage we can detect is that his mother was a woman of quite outstanding faith and courage.

It seems that Joseph, Jesus' earthly father, died while Jesus was quite young. But not before he had passed on to his son the skills of carpentry; and Jesus must have worked for many years to support his mother, brothers and sisters. He knew what it felt like to have sawdust in his eye, or painstakingly to fit a yoke to an ox.

When he left the north-country town of Nazareth and moved into public life, Jesus emerged as a truly good person with an astonishing concern for the bad and the ugly. He plunged into the company of the suspect tax collectors and despised prostitutes, sharing their meals and enjoying their parties. The religious leaders of the day watched him and were appalled at what they saw.

Jesus took no notice at all of the lines of race, wealth and class which every society so carefully draws. With startling independence, he could hold a private conversation with a ruling Pharisee at midnight, or talk to a notorious woman (and a Samaritan one at that) at noon. He broke down other barriers as well, touching the untouchable and loving the unlovely.

When Jesus walked this earth, he

experienced the whole of life. Like all of us, he got tired and hot at times. Like all of us, he got hungry and thirsty, angry and frustrated. Like all of us, he had times of the utmost elation and joy. There was something very ordinary about him: he was fully human. And yet he was extraordinary in that he was 'complete'. He was fully human in the way that God intended us to be, but which no one else in the history of the world has ever managed.

In his Gospel, John described Jesus as 'the Word', and said this of him:

The Word became a human being and, full of grace and truth, lived among us. We saw his glory, the glory which he received as the Father's only Son.

In his letter to the Philippians, the apostle Paul paid tribute to Jesus in this way:

He always had the nature of God, but he did not think that by force he

God is not remote from our human lives. He has got involved with us; he knows what life is like

should try to become equal with God. Instead of this, of his own free will he gave up all he had, and took the nature of a servant. He became like man and appeared in human likeness. He was humble and walked the path of obedience all the way to death: his death on the cross.

All this means that Jesus was deeply and movingly committed to reaching humanity. He did not come to think great thoughts, write fine books, or train good people. He came to plumb the very depths of human misery and despair. He came to make contact, literally, with the sick, diseased, and disabled members of society. Even more wonderfully, he came to share God's love and forgiveness with the rich, the proud and the self-satisfied.

He came for us all, because he loves us all. And he laid down his life for us all, so that we may come back to God through him.

Come to me, all of you who are tired from carrying heavy loads, and I will give you rest. Take my yoke and put it on you, and learn from me, because I am gentle and humble in spirit; and you will find rest. For the yoke I will give you is easy, and the load I will put on you is light.

MATTHEW'S GOSPEL CHAPTER 11

KNOWING THE FATHER

How did Jesus manage to live such an unselfish and outgoing life?

His secret was prayer. It was in prayer that he basked in his Father's love. Prayer was as important to him as breathing.

Early in the morning, or in the quiet hours of the night, he would find a secluded place to spend time with his Father in heaven. We glimpse him praying about the direction of his work, about his choice of disciples, and about his fear of the cross...

Each of us needs to be loved. Without love, something in us dies. If we are fortunate, we find that love in our parents, our partners, our children, or our friends.

For Jesus, this love came from his face-to-face relationship with God. It was in prayer that he found himself to be most truly God's Son. It was such a deep sense of wellbeing and belonging that he called it 'abiding'. He felt nourished by the Father's love. He felt strengthened, his batteries recharged. And he could say to his disciples with simple conviction, 'I am in the Father and the Father is in me.' Or, 'The Father and I are one.'

It was in prayer that Jesus discovered more of who he was, and more of what he had come to do. He had been sent by his Father to be 'the light of the world', 'the living

The prayer of Jesus

The balance of Jesus' life is beautifully stated in the prayer he taught his disciples:

Father:

May your holy Name be honoured;
may your Kingdom come.
Give us day by day the food we need.
Forgive us our sins,
for we forgive everyone who does us wrong.
And do not bring us to hard testing.
LUKE'S GOSPEL CHAPTER 11

Praying my own prayer

We are all different. And surely there are as many ways of praying as there are people to pray!

At first we may copy someone else, or use the prayers in a particular book. We may find it helpful to pray with others, or perhaps we prefer to take ourselves off to our own special place.

The important thing to remember is that only *you* can come to God your way, and only *you* can pray your prayer. And it's the *real* you – the call from *your* heart – that God hears.

bread', and 'the water of life'. But despite this supreme status, he went about his work without a shred of pride or self-seeking. On the contrary, the hallmark of his life was self-giving love. He had come to be poured out. As Mark's Gospel records:

The Son of Man did not come to be served; he came to serve and give his life to redeem many people.

Because the whole of his life was a prayer, Jesus had a perfect balance of taking in from God and giving out to others. Despite the constant pressures on him to heal and help, he held fast to the conviction that he had only to do his Father's will: no more and no less. There were undoubtedly some heavy days and some long nights, but Jesus was always alert to the dangers of getting over-stretched. He went out of his way to secure times of rest and refreshment both for his disciples and for himself: times when they could regain God's perspective, and halt the stampede of overwork and strain.

12

TELLING IT STRAIGHT

Jesus was a great teacher. His sayings and stories were always gripping, often amusing, and invariably true. They opened up a view of life and an understanding of God which put the whole landscape of this world in an entirely new light.

He led with the truth. And his truth set people free.

When he wanted to describe the kingdom of God, he plucked everyday pictures from all directions. To belong to God's kingdom is the greatest treasure we can have, and it's worth giving up anything and everything else to obtain it. It's like a labourer finding treasure in a field, and going off to cash his house, contents and all, to buy the land.

But then again, the kingdom of God isn't so much a treasure we save for as an invitation we accept. Never mind if we've disgraced ourselves, like a son running away from home and squandering his father's fortune; if only we turn back to God and ask for his new start, he'll welcome us in!

Asking, seeking, knocking

Jesus' way of prayer may seem far beyond our own feeble efforts. But he invites us to join him all the same. He urges us to see that God is our loving Father, and to bring him our deepest longings and heartfelt needs.

And the Jesus method is by no means remote, exotic or exclusive. He doesn't lead us to God via transcendental meditation, drugs, or even relaxation exercises. Rather he says, 'God knows you through and through. He loves you completely. So don't be afraid to ask.'

And so I say to you: Ask, and you will receive; seek, and you will find; knock, and the door will be opened to you. For everyone who asks will receive, and he who seeks will find, and the door will be opened to anyone who knocks.

Is there any restriction on what we should ask?

Well, the best things will always be those which God himself is longing to give us. Most of all, he waits to bless us with the gift of his own Spirit. In the eleventh chapter of Luke's Gospel Jesus continues:

Would any of you who are fathers give your son a snake when he asks for fish? Or would you give him a scorpion when he asks for an egg? Bad as you are, you know how to give good gifts to your children. How much more, then, will the Father in heaven give the Holy Spirit to those who ask him!

Ordinary people were attracted to Jesus and intrigued by what he had to say. He was good, but he wasn't a pious prig. He was fun to be with. He honoured God's law, but he wasn't a tight-lipped legalist. And he wasn't so busy thinking deep thoughts and indulging in clever debates that he couldn't drop everything and attend to the needs of those around him.

The words of Jesus were matched by his whole life. No one knew this better than his group of disciples. For them, the Jesus way was 'caught' rather than 'taught'. They were with him round the clock for many months of talking and travelling, preaching and healing. Their verdict was that Jesus was genuine, Jesus was authentic. One of the disciples, John, in his old age wrote in one of his letters:

The way to freedom

Jesus said 'If you obey my teaching, you are really my disciples; you will know the truth, and the truth will set you free.'

JOHN'S GOSPEL CHAPTER 8

Happy are they

The heart of Jesus' teaching about behaviour is to be found in the Sermon on the Mount. In just three chapters of Matthew's Gospel (chapters 5, 6 and 7), we have the clearest, deepest and most searching sayings the world has ever heard.

With masterly simplicity, Jesus sums up the whole Jewish law (and there was a lot of it!) in the twin command to love God whole heartedly and to love our fellow men and women (including our enemies) as we love ourselves.

He gives us the key to all right behaviour: that we should obey God because we love him, and seek to approach life with a pure heart.

At every point, it's the heart that counts! By 'heart' Jesus means that part of ourselves where all our deepest loves and loathings are concentrated. In other words, the teaching of Jesus starts from the inside, tackling and changing what's in us, and then working outwards to change the things we do. This is completely different from every other kind of law-making, which heaps up rules and regulations to govern our behaviour, but gets nowhere near the source of the trouble.

Our problem, as Jesus knows so well, is not what we *do* but what we *are*. It is what we *are* that Jesus came to change.

We have heard the Word of life. We have seen it with our eyes; yes, we have seen it, and our hands have touched it. When this life became visible, we saw it; so we speak of it and tell you about the eternal life which was with the Father and was made known to us. What we have seen and heard we announce to you also, so that you will join with us in the fellowship that we have with the Father and with his Son Jesus Christ.

With most teachers, their classes and lectures may be impressive enough, but the rest of their life lets them down. Even the finest preachers are only human. At the end of the day they can only point to Jesus as our example, and not to themselves.

But Jesus was different. He could say without a shadow of doubt or a tremor of hypocrisy, 'I am the way, the truth, and the life.'

MENDING PEOPLE

Jesus taught people about the kingdom of God. But he did more than that. He showed the kingdom of God in action. He went around

Happy are those who know they are spiritually poor; the Kingdom of heaven belongs to them!
Happy are those who mourn; God will comfort them!

Happy are those who are humble; they will receive what God has promised!
Happy are those whose greatest desire is to do what God requires; God will satisfy them fully!
Happy are those who are merciful to others; God will be merciful to them!
Happy are the pure in heart; they will see God!
Happy are those who work for peace; God will call them his children!
Happy are those who are persecuted because they do what God requires; the Kingdom of heaven belongs to them!
Happy are you when people insult you and persecute you and tell all kinds of evil lies against you because you are my followers.

MATTHEW'S GOSPEL CHAPTER 5

mending people. He made them whole in body, mind and spirit.

Jesus healed all kinds of people. He restored sight to the blind, hearing to the deaf, and strength to those who were crippled. Many times he gave sanity and peace of mind by casting out evil spirits. Even his enemies and critics had to agree that he was an outstanding healer and exorcist, for they could not deny the facts.

But there was a special ingredient in the healings of Jesus. That ingredient was faith. Faith in God's power to heal. And where that faith was missing, Jesus was powerless.

When a woman who had been bleeding for many years fought her way through a crowd to tug Jesus' robe, she was immediately healed. But Jesus was at pains to explain to her that there was nothing magic about his clothes. It was her faith in God that had made her well.

This shows that the healing of Jesus was concerned with the whole person. There was no point in tinkering with symptoms if people were at odds with God in their hearts. When a paralysed man was lowered through the roof by his friends, so that Jesus could heal him, Jesus was careful to deal first with the man's sin. Only after he knew that God had forgiven him could he enjoy the healing of his paralysis.

And Jesus was never sensational. He would often urge people to go quietly about their lives, simply enjoying the wholeness and peace that God had given them. His typical farewell was, 'Go in peace, your faith has made you whole.'

Good news

When Jesus taught, ordinary people found they could understand him. What's more, they found they could believe what he said. Something was coming out of him which was true, strong and clear. Time after time people commented, 'He speaks with authority.'

And yet he said some astonishing things. His first sermon in the synagogue at Nazareth scandalized his neighbours, as he took some words from the prophet Isaiah and applied them directly to himself:

'The Spirit of the Lord is upon me, because he has chosen me to bring good news to the poor. He has sent me to proclaim liberty to the captives and recovery of sight to the blind; to set free the oppressed and announce that the time has come when the Lord will save his people'.

LUKE'S GOSPEL CHAPTER 4

The congregation were so shocked that, as soon as they recovered, they tried to throw him over a cliff. But no one had the power to harm him yet. His work was only just beginning.

The healing power of Jesus' love can transform even the darkest parts of our lives

PERFECTLY ANGRY

Jesus preached love and showed love. But that doesn't mean he never got irritated. And on occasions he was thoroughly angry.

What kind of thing made him see red?

The most famous episode was when he took a whip and cleared the temple courtyard of all the traders and moneychangers. He was incensed that a place of pilgrimage and prayer had been invaded and overrun by greedy and dishonest dealers. But this was no spontaneous loss of temper. Mark tells us that Jesus had visited the temple the previous day and had a good look round. It was only after he had thought deeply and slept on his decision that he made up his mind to act in this way.

Another thing Jesus loathed was hypocrisy – people pretending to be something they weren't. This was a criticism he levelled at many of the religious leaders of the day, and he didn't mince his words. He called them 'blind guides' and 'sons of hell'!

So far as Jesus was concerned, the Pharisees had turned the Jewish religion on its head. By multiplying God's law into hundreds of petty rules and regulations, they had turned the high road of faith into a forest of legalism.

Jesus saw so clearly that they were just playing games. They

Healing today

Does God heal through Jesus today?

Yes, he does.

In God's eyes, we all need help. Even those who are fully fit in body and mind still need the forgiveness of sins, the cleansing of guilt, the healing of memories, the mending of relationships.

Many people can say that God has healed their sickness or disability. Others are still quietly and confidently looking to God to heal them. All have the assurance that, in Paul's words, 'To live is Christ, and to die is gain.' If it is through death that God chooses to heal us, taking us to be with him, then that is a wonderful deliverance too.

God's healing is always complete. It never removes one symptom only to allow another to spring up elsewhere.

God's healing always includes forgiveness and peace of mind, whether or not the illness itself disappears.

God's healing always draws the person closer to Jesus, and gives a special radiance and understanding to his or her life.

were washing their hands very nicely before every meal, and making sure their cups and bowls were clean, but at the bottom of it all was pride. They were proud of their cast iron routine – the routine that keep them on the right side of God, or so they thought.

Jesus confronted them with words from the prophet Isaiah:

These people ... honour me with their words, but their heart is really far away from me.

Their religion was just a front. It was nothing to do with loving God and serving him. Indeed, while God in his love welcomes people into his kingdom, the Pharisees were very busy ensuring that most people stayed out!

In the Sermon on the Mount (Matthew's Gospel chapter 5), Jesus took them once again to the heart of God's law. If the commandment said 'Don't murder', then that included 'Don't be angry with people, and don't abuse them'. It's the heart that counts. God wants us to be forgiving, as we have been forgiven by him.

If the commandment says 'Don't commit adultery', then that includes our thoughts and fantasies. It includes the 'come on' we give with our eyes, or the suggestive words we say. Again, it's the heart that counts.

As for the whole attitude of living by the exact letter of the law ('an eye for an eye, and a tooth for a tooth'), Jesus opened up a radical alternative. When we are wronged,

we shouldn't seek revenge. When we are on the receiving end of bullying, anger or exploitation, we should accept it and take it out of circulation. Jesus said:

Do not take revenge on someone who wrongs you. If anyone slaps you on the right cheek, let him slap your left cheek too. And if someone takes you to court to sue you for your shirt, let him have your coat as well. And if one of the occupation troops forces you to carry his pack one kilometre, carry it two kilometres. When someone asks you for something, give it to him; when someone wants to borrow something, lend it to him.

And Jesus had a bone to pick with people who made a big show of their prayers, their fasting, and giving to charity. They tended to do such things in public places, so that people would be sure to see them. But Jesus said such activities should be secret:

When you give something to a needy person, do not make a big show of it, as the hypocrites do in the houses of worship and on the streets ... When you help a needy person, do it in such a way that even your closest friend will not know about it. Then it will be a private matter. And your Father who sees what you do in private, will reward you ...

When you pray, go to your room, close the door, and pray to your Father, who is unseen. And your Father, who sees what you do in private, will reward you.

Once Jesus described his good news as like 'new wine'. But the new wine was being poured into the stiff leather bottles of Jewish legalism. There could only be one result: the bottles would burst. Or again, it was like a fully shrunk garment being patched with unshrunk cloth: the patch would rip away.

LEADING BY SERVING

At the height of his popularity, Jesus had considerable public support. He could easily have raised an army, proclaimed himself king, and marched on Jerusalem. This was what the Jewish leaders dreaded. It was also the dearest hope of many a disciple's heart!

Jesus' disciples often used to dream of the power that would be theirs when Jesus came to the throne. More than once we catch snatches of their conversation as they trudge the dusty roads behind Jesus. The nearer they got to Jerusalem, the more they bickered about who would be most important in the new kingdom. For his part, Jesus constantly tried to tell them that armed rebellion and power politics were not his way. He would lead by serving. He would save by dying.

On one occasion he explained:

You know that the men who are considered rulers of the heathen have power over them, and the leaders have complete authority. This, however, is not the way it is among you. If one of you wants to be great, he must be the servant of the rest; and if one of you wants to be first, he must be the slave of all. For even the Son of Man did not come to be served; he came to serve and to give his life to redeem many people.

MARK'S GOSPEL CHAPTER 10

Francis of Assisi

Throughout history, Christians have tried to follow Jesus in caring for 'the poorest of the poor'. Early on in his commitment to Christ, Francis was confronted by a leper. Normally he would have put spurs to his horse and galloped away, but as a Christian he was overcome by compassion instead.

Putting aside the fear and disgust of a lifetime, he dismounted from his horse, walked up to the beggar, gave him some money, and then slowly and deliberately kissed his hand.

A day or two later, he visited the leper house and went round to each of the sufferers, embracing them and giving them help. Years later, he still looked on this episode as one of the most important turning points of his life.

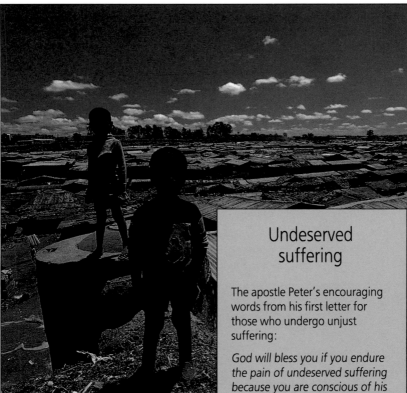

Undeserved suffering

The apostle Peter's encouraging words from his first letter for those who undergo unjust suffering:

God will bless you if you endure the pain of undeserved suffering because you are conscious of his will. For what credit is there if you endure the beatings you deserve for having done wrong? But if you endure suffering even when you have done right, God will bless you for it. It was to this that God called you, for Christ himself suffered for you and left you an example, so that you would follow in his steps. He committed no sin, and no one ever heard a lie come from his lips. When he was insulted, he did not answer back with an insult; when he suffered, he did not threaten, but placed his hopes in God, the righteous Judge.

On the night before he died, Jesus impressed this lesson on them once again. While they were eating supper, he took off his robe, took a bowl of water and a towel, and washed the feet of each of his disciples. It was the job of a slave, and his friends found it both shocking and embarrassing. And yet it showed them, in a single gesture, the kind of Lord he came to be. The kind of intimate understanding and cleansing he came to give.

Jesus came to Simon Peter, who said to him, 'Are you going to wash my feet, Lord?'

Jesus answered him, 'You do not understand now what I am doing, but you will understand later.'

Peter declared, 'Never at any time will you wash my feet!'

'If I do not wash your feet,' Jesus answered, 'you will no longer be my disciple.'

Simon Peter answered, 'Lord, do not wash only my feet, then! Wash my hands and head, too!' ...

After Jesus had washed their feet, he put his outer garments back on and returned to his place at the table. 'Do you understand what I have just done to you?' he asked. 'You call me Teacher and Lord, and it is right that you do so, because that is what I am. I, your Lord and Teacher, have just washed your feet. You, then, should wash one another's feet.

JOHN'S GOSPEL CHAPTER 13

GOING UNDER

Whenever the disciples were getting high on their ideas of sorting out the Jews and throwing

The quality of Jesus' life and character represents humanity at its highest – life as God meant it to be. Yet this level of life is not remote and distant from us. Jesus promised to help and guide us, by his Spirit

Taking in and giving out

'Whoever believes in me,' said Jesus, 'streams of living water will flow from within him.' Jesus drew his strength from his Father, and was able to give himself unstintingly to others. His followers, too, need to take in from God if they are to serve the world without physical, mental and spiritual exhaustion.

Jesus was constantly aware of his Father's love: 'You are my dear Son.'

Jesus lived, not for himself, but for others; 'The Son of Man did not come to be served, but to serve.'

renounced all other tactics – flashy miracles, sensational stunts during the temptations at the start of his ministry. He knew that, instead, he must suffer every kind of degradation plumbing the very depths of all that is wrong with the world. He was to be killed in the crash of the world running away from God.

And yet Jesus' death was at the heart of God's plan to save us. When Jesus gave up his life on the cross, it was God himself disappearing under the waves of sin and death. The death of Jesus was the loving sacrifice prepared, shared and accepted by God. And beyond it lay the resurrection morning, the joy of God's victory, and the gate of heaven wide open for us all.

out the Romans, Jesus would have solemn words for them. He would remind them that his was a hard road, and that he was under sentence of death.

Listen, we are going up to Jerusalem where the Son of Man will be handed over to the chief priest and the teachers of the Law. They will condemn him to death and then hand him over to the Gentiles, who will mock him, spit on him, whip him, and kill him; but three days later he will rise to life.

MARK'S GOSPEL CHAPTER 10

All along, Jesus was aware of the suffering that lay ahead. He had

LIVING ONE LIFE AND LIVING IT IN THE OPEN

Was there ever an age when people talked about peace and love and freedom more than we do or knew less about them?

But when we look at Jesus, we can define peace and love and freedom perfectly. And not just in terms of theory, but in terms of a life lived, of words said, of deeds done.

Jesus spells peace. Jesus spells love. Jesus spells freedom.

Whether he was dining with his disciples, pausing to heal a blind beggar, talking to the woman at the well, or standing on trial before Pontius Pilate, he seemed to know all the failings and feeble hopes that we share. But he always looked past the sin (which he hated) to the real person (whom he loved). He saw the faint glimmer of what each could become when warmed by the love of God, granted his forgiveness, and drawn into his peace.

Jesus lived a particular life in a particular time and place. But the example he gave can be lived out everywhere and in every age. His words are eternally true.

He shows us the simplicity and zest of a life open to God. Without a home, and with only one coat (unless someone else needed it), he shows that real wealth is nothing to do with possessions. By the way he accepted misunderstandings, hostility, and interruptions, he shows the exciting breakthrough of saying 'No' to ourselves. It's the true way of life, always, and in all circumstances.

Jesus was open to God. And because he was open to God, he was open to others. So he could discover signs of God's kingdom all around, and he himself was free to share the healing power of the kingdom life.

FROM SMALL BEGINNINGS

Where do we get the strength to follow Jesus?
Christianity is not just trying to imitate Christ.
The good news is that he gives us his own
power and love

STARTING FROM WHERE WE ARE

Something in us longs to start over again. Every birthday, every New Year, every Monday morning...

Of course, we are not short of ideas. Scientists and sociologists, politicians and planners, all offer a brave new world of our choice. But somehow it never works out. Somehow it is always spoiled by people like us.

Oh yes, we can look around for someone to blame. It's in our stars, in our background, in our bloodstream. The workers blame the management, the management blames the government, the government blames the world. But at the end of the day we must call our own bluff. We must stop pointing the finger elsewhere or making excuses. And we must put the blame fairly and squarely where it belongs. On ourselves. On human nature.

Our problem is that we sin. We can no more stop sinning than a spider can stop spinning webs. When we try to be good, we fail. When we devise right rules, we break them. If we sense the warmth of temptation, we home in on wrongdoing like a heat seeking missile.

We try to shrug off our failure. 'It's a temporary setback.' 'It'll be all right in the end.' 'I'll never do it again.' 'Anyway, I'm not as bad as all that. I know people far worse.'

The key to it all

After Jesus was so cruelly put to death, God raised his Son from the grave. Not reviving him for a few more years, but raising him to eternal life in heaven.

The life of Jesus was a crucial victory over sin. The resurrection of Jesus was the decisive conquest of death. On the cross, Jesus established a bridgehead between earth and heaven, between us and God.

When we put our trust in Jesus we have a new start.

But if we really believe that we're basically good, we're fooling ourselves. Certainly we can make short-term improvements. We can turn over a new leaf – check a bad habit, control our language, and inflict a burst of kindness on our friends. But all these are just minor adjustments. Our heart disease remains. We've tackled the symptoms, but not the cause.

When Jesus diagnosed our spiritual disease, he traced it to the heart the 'self':

We live at odds with those around us, we live with stress and worry; there's an emptiness we feel inside – our lives are spoiled by sin. How can we make a fresh start?

From the inside, from a person's heart, come the evil ideas which lead him to do immoral things, to rob, kill, commit adultery, be greedy, and do all sorts of evil things; deceit, indecency, jealousy, slander, pride, and folly – all these evil things come from inside a person and make him unclean.

MARK'S GOSPEL CHAPTER 7

So this is a cancer which is inside us all. It has taken up residence in human nature. It's not like a disease which some catch and some don't. We've all caught it. And we're all guilty.

We notice the effects of sin all the time:

● **We are anti-God**

We doubt his existence, deny his goodness, and defy his law.

● **We are at odds with others**

Even with our closest family and friends, we are too often selfish, angry, jealous or unkind.

27

'When anyone is joined to Christ, he is a new being; the old is gone, the new has come.'

• We live in a mess

Our attempts at building community are balked by the self seeking of some and the suspicion of others. Our greed leads us to ransack the earth's resources, and pollute the environment. Our pent up rage keeps the world tense and the nations divided.

A NEW START

When we put our trust in Jesus we have a new start. We leave our old life with him on the cross, enjoy his triumph over sin and death, and begin to taste and share the life of heaven.

It's like waking up to sunshine; it's like coming out of prison; it's like being born again.

The message of the Bible is summed up in these marvellous words from John's Gospel:

God loved the world so much that he gave his only Son, so that everyone who believes in him may not die but have eternal life.

When Jesus died so painfully on the cross, he took the punishment and paid the penalty for our sins. He provided a black hole into which our filth and failure can be thrown and never seen again. He opened up a way for us to be right with God giving us the fresh air of his Spirit in this life, and a home in heaven for all eternity.

That's why we call Jesus our 'Saviour'. He came to do for us what we could never do for ourselves. He offers forgiveness for our past, his exhilarating friendship in the present, and a glorious confidence and hope for the future.

Of course, Jesus is a realist. He knows us through and through. He knows the selfishness and pride of our human nature, and the enormous difficulties that we face. But his power is a match for all these things. In his strength, we can put the past behind. However dreadful our life has been, it is forgiven and forgotten. God no longer remembers it, and all we have left are the scars. We need never go back to that old life again, for we are living in a new dimension altogether.

Like a butterfly emerging from a chrysalis, the Christian changes into something completely different. Paul's shorthand for explaining our new life was to say that we are 'in Christ'. In his second letter to the Corinthians, he put it this way:

When anyone is joined to Christ, he

New life

New life in Jesus is God's free gift. We didn't dream it up, we didn't earn it, and we certainly don't deserve it! It doesn't even depend on whether we feel we've got it. God gives us his new life, born out of love, bought on the cross, offered free in Jesus.
And now that I have accepted Jesus I am free to learn how to live the Jesus life.
Whatever life may hold, I am his and he is mine. So relax!

is a new being; the old is gone, the new has come.

And many millions of people from Paul's time to the present day have found this to be true. They have found that, trusting in what Jesus has done for them, they have enjoyed a new openness to God, a new love for others, and a whole new patience, courage and hope in times of trouble. For every Christian there is the freedom and zest that comes only from knowing that God loves us, our sins are forgiven, and our life belongs to him.

UNDER NEW MANAGEMENT

When we start out with Jesus, we are under new management. Jesus is not just our Saviour, he is also our Lord. We are members of his family. We are playing in his team. We are fighting on his side.

In our old life, we were hopelessly hooked on sin. No efforts of our own could spring us from the prison of self-centredness or avert the finality of death. But when Jesus came, he mounted a superb rescue operation.

Now we belong to Jesus. He is our new Master. All that we are and all that we have belongs to him. It's the most joyful commitment we can possibly make.

For one thing, his service is perfect freedom. We are free from

guilt. We are free to do right. We are free to give our lives in the loving service of others, in a way which would have been unthinkable before.

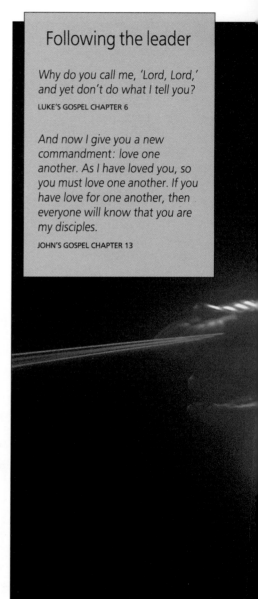

Following the leader

Why do you call me, 'Lord, Lord,' and yet don't do what I tell you?
LUKE'S GOSPEL CHAPTER 6

And now I give you a new commandment: love one another. As I have loved you, so you must love one another. If you have love for one another, then everyone will know that you are my disciples.
JOHN'S GOSPEL CHAPTER 13

And secondly, although Jesus is our Lord, he never at any time treats us as slaves. On the contrary, he counts us as his friends. He is totally committed to our well being, our personal growth, and our success in the Christian life. We serve Jesus because we want to, because he has won our hearts, because we owe him our life, because we love him.

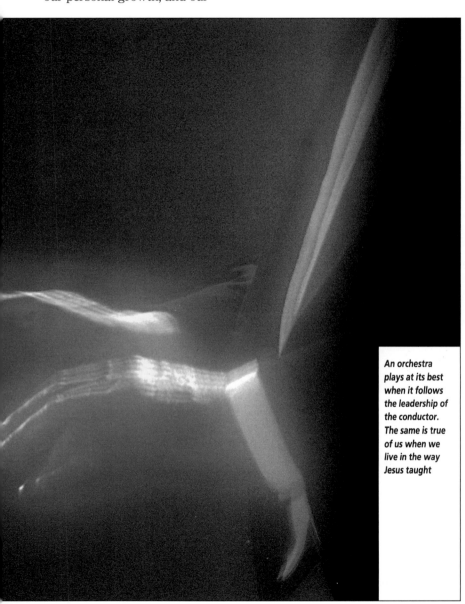

An orchestra plays at its best when it follows the leadership of the conductor. The same is true of us when we live in the way Jesus taught

POWER TO ALL HIS FRIENDS

God is Spirit invisible, but personal and powerful. We can't see or touch him, but we are surrounded by the evidence of his existence and without him we would cease to be. Wherever there is healing, harmony and love – that's the Spirit!

When Jesus walked this earth, the Holy Spirit of God was upon him in a complete and beautiful way. Those who watched him teaching and healing were seeing God at work in the lives of men and women. And when the time came for Jesus to return to heaven, he promised that the same Spirit that was in him would be given to his followers.

The Christian life is not about trying harder! It's not about trying to love God, trying to love other people, or trying to do better. Indeed, it's not about trying at all!

Like the wind, the Holy Spirit cannot be seen. But, also like the wind, the effects of the Holy Spirit's presence have visible results

The Christian life is all to do with letting the Spirit of Jesus live in us. The apostle Paul put it this way in his letter to the Galatians:

I have been put to death with Christ on his cross, so that it is no longer I who live, but it is Christ who lives in me. This life that I live now, I live by faith in the Son of God, who loved me and gave his life for me.

The Holy Spirit is our power base. We rely on it for our spiritual life as we rely on fresh air for our physical life. Without the Spirit of Jesus we are as helpless as a fish out of water, and as useless as a yacht without wind. But with the Holy Spirit, we are in our element! The Holy Spirit assures us that God is our loving Father, and that Jesus is his Son. It enables us to say not only, 'Jesus is the Lord,' but 'Jesus is *our* Lord'.

Like the wind, the Holy Spirit cannot be seen. But we can certainly see the effects of his presence, and the differences he makes. The Holy Spirit is with us at every stage of our Christian life; was the midwife who brought us into new life with God when we were born again; is our life-giving teacher who makes it possible for us to develop spiritually; helps us praise and pray, and share our faith with others. Without the Holy Spirit, both worship and witness would be impossible.

Jesus called the Holy Spirit Helper, Comforter, or Counsellor – the one who stands with us, supports us and advises us in every situation.

GIFTS AND FRUIT

The Holy Spirit gives special gifts to Christian people, to build up the life of the church. Such a gift is never something to be proud of (like a trophy or badge), but something to be gladly used in serving others. A spiritual gift is always for sharing! Paul talks about some of

Gifts and love must go together

The Christians at Corinth had experience of many spiritual gifts. But Paul wrote in his first letter to tell them that unless those gifts were received and used in Christian love, they would be spoiled by pride, jealousy and squabbles:

I may be able to speak the languages of men and even of angels, but if I have no love, my speech is no more than a noisy gong or a clanging bell. I may have all knowledge and understand all secrets; I may have all the faith needed to move mountains but if I have no love, I am nothing. I may give away everything I have, and even give up my body to be burnt but if I have no love, this does me no good.

Love is patient and kind; it is not jealous or conceited or proud; love is not ill mannered or selfish or irritable; love is not happy with evil, but is happy with the truth. Love never gives up; and its faith, hope and patience never fail.

> *As Christians, we should be much more like fruit trees than Christmas trees – not with spiritual decorations tied on us from outside, but with the fruit of a Christlike life growing from within.*

and to another he gives the ability to explain what is said.

But having mentioned just some of the gifts of the Spirit, Paul is eager to point out that gifted Christians belong together and need each other like limbs and organs in the body of Christ:

Christ is like a single body, which has many parts ... If the foot were to say, 'Because I am not a hand, I don't belong to the body,' that would not keep it from being a part of the body. And if the ear were to say, 'Because I am not an eye, I don't belong to the body,' that would not keep it from being a part of the body. If the whole body were just an eye, how could it hear? And if it were only an ear, how could it smell? As it is, however, God put every different part in the body just as he wanted it to be ... All of you are Christ's body, and each one is part of it.

them in his second letter to the Corinthians:

The Spirit gives one person a message full of wisdom, while to another person the same Spirit gives a message full of knowledge. One and the same Spirit gives faith to one person, while to another person he gives the power to heal. The Spirit gives one person the power to work miracles; to another, the gift of speaking God's message; and to yet another, the ability to tell the difference between gifts that come from the Spirit and those that do not. To one person he gives the ability to speak in strange tongues,

No one can be blamed for not possessing a particular spiritual gift. Gifts come from God, and he decides what he gives and to whom. All the same, every Christian has at least one. Paul wrote to the Romans:

If our gift is to speak God's message, we should do it according to the faith that we have; if it is to serve, we should serve; if it is to teach, we should teach; if it is to encourage others, we should do so. Whoever shares with others should do it generously; whoever has authority should work hard; whoever shows kindness to others should do it cheerfully.

35

And there is certainly no room for jealousy. If another Christian has a gift we would like, then we can give thanks to God that he has blessed that person with a view to blessing us all.

No one in the world possesses all the spiritual gifts, but every Christian can be bearing spiritual fruit. Paul describes the fruit of the Spirit in this way in his letter to the Galatians:

The Spirit produces love, joy, peace, patience, kindness, goodness, faithfulness, humility, and self-control.

In other words, he describes nine aspects of the Jesus life which can develop in each of us without exception.

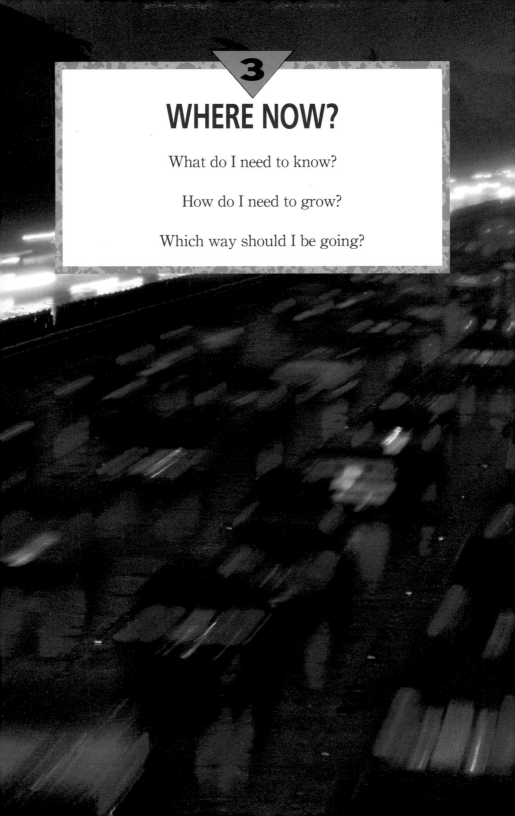

WHERE NOW?

What do I need to know?

How do I need to grow?

Which way should I be going?

WHAT STAGE AM I AT?

When I become a Christian, a new life begins for me.

Some people feel this new life immediately. The whole world seems to be in glorious technicolor, where before it was merely grey. For some it's like a whole new horizon opening up, where before their world view was narrow and blinkered.

Again, some people feel nothing at all! They know they have crossed a frontier, but at first the landscape seems little different. Never mind. With or without feelings, we are going in a new direction. We are on our way with God.

The first and greatest difference is going to be in our behaviour. This is what we would expect and it is certainly what our friends expect!

- **We have turned away from evil and are following Jesus.**

- **We want to grow in our understanding of what it is to be a Christian and to enjoy listening to God and responding to his voice.**

- **We want to discover how we belong to the wider Christian family and to play our part as fully as possible.**

- **We want to find God's purpose for our lives so that we can invest our time and talents in his service.**

BLOW UP YOUR TV!

In his song 'Spanish Pipe-dream', John Prine captures the joy of a changed life:

Blow up your TV!
Throw away your paper!
Move to the country; build a home.
Have a little garden;
Grow a lot of peaches!
Try and find Jesus
On your own.

Well, that's repentance! Changing your mind about something, and then going on to change your way of life.

The Christian life begins with

repentance. Not in terms of blowing up the TV, throwing away the paper, or even growing peaches. But in terms of turning right around from our old direction. We are no longer going our own way. Instead, we are following Jesus.

● **Repentance is the starting point**

The only starting point for those who want to live the Jesus life. It is given to those who come empty-handed and open hearted to God, to ask his forgiveness of their sins. And it is followed by the most marvellous sense of relief and joy.

How strange that repentance, which sounds so morbid and woebegone, should turn out to be so exhilarating!

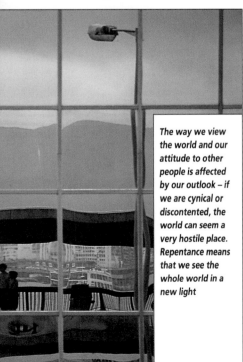

The way we view the world and our attitude to other people is affected by our outlook – if we are cynical or discontented, the world can seem a very hostile place. Repentance means that we see the whole world in a new light

● **Repentance includes a prayer**

I will say to God, in my own words and in my own way, that I am sorry. Sorry for what I have been, and sorry for what I have done. I humbly ask him to let me start over again. I invite Jesus to come into my life to be my Lord.

● **Repentance will include baptism**

This is the public bath or wash which Jesus chose to be the sign of our change of heart and the beginning of our new life in God's family. If you were brought up in a church which baptizes babies, you can thank God that the things which were said and done for you as a child are now real in your own experience. Many Christians prefer to keep baptism for adults, and you may feel very deeply that you want to be baptized again. If so, then talk to your pastor or minister about it and go ahead! It will be a public sign of your commitment to Christ, and will bring glory to God.

● **Repentance means making changes**

There may be something very wrong in your life that you have to put right. You may have to break a bad habit, put an end to a wrong relationship, give back something you have stolen, or apologize to someone you have hurt.

When Zacchaeus the taxman accepted the good news of Jesus for himself, he said, 'I will give half my belongings to the poor, and if I have cheated anyone, I will pay him back four times as much.' To which Jesus replied, 'Salvation has come to this

house today!' (Luke's Gospel chapter 19)

● **Repentance means seeing the whole world in a new light**

If before you thought that life was meaningless, now you know that it is the gift of a wise and loving Creator. If before your main aim was to please yourself, now you know that you live to please God. You have Jesus as the best friend imaginable, and you have the rest of your days (and indeed eternity) to enjoy his company.

BECOMING WHAT WE ARE

Becoming a Christian just takes a moment. Being a Christian takes a lifetime. Even if I have only been a Christian two minutes, the Bible refers to me as a saint! That's because in the Bible a saint isn't a figure in a stained glass window, nor is it someone who goes out of his way to be kind. No, a saint, so far as the Bible is concerned, is someone who has been made holy

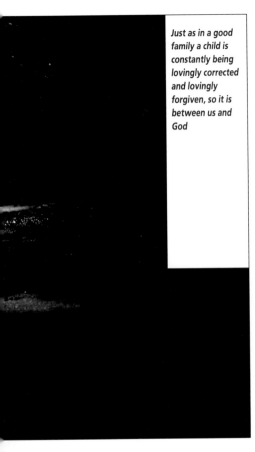

Just as in a good family a child is constantly being lovingly corrected and lovingly forgiven, so it is between us and God

Corinthian Christians:

You have been purified from sin...
You have been put right with God.

And yet in his second letter to them he invites:

So then, let us purify ourselves from everything that makes body or soul unclean, and let us be completely holy by living in awe of God.

So the truth is that we *are* already completely Christian, but there is always room for improvement! Being a saint is a process, rather than a finished product.

● Being a Christian means being sure of God's love

In his first letter, the apostle John wrote, 'See how much the Father has loved us! His love is so great that we are called God's children and so, in fact, we are.' We are God's children! We can come to him with our every need. We can say 'our Father' with freshness, intimacy, and love.

● Being a Christian means being forgiven

Even when we are wilful and disobedient children (as no doubt we will be, from time to time), we can ask our Father for forgiveness. We may get on the wrong side of him, but nothing will ever change the fact that we are still his children. In that same letter, John writes, 'If we say that we have no sin, we deceive ourselves, and there is no truth in us. But if we confess our sins to God, he will keep his promise and do what is right: he

('holified') *in Christ Jesus*. It isn't what anyone has *done*, but rather what Jesus has been allowed to do in and for that person.

Holiness is given to us by God. It is something of himself which he shares with us, because we are his people – his family.

We can't earn holiness by hard work. We can't win holiness by good fortune. We can only receive it as a gift.

All the same, it is something in which we can grow. Paul shows us both sides of the same coin when he writes in his first letter to the will forgive us our sins and purify us from all our wrongdoing.'

Not one of us is perfect. The chances are that we will sadden or disappoint God every day of our lives, and perhaps many times a day. But just as in a family a child is constantly being lovingly corrected and lovingly forgiven, so it is between us and God.

● **Being a Christian also means taking Jesus at his word**

And his solemn promise is, 'I will never turn away anyone who comes to me.'

Our feelings may vary, but that doesn't matter. If we have come to him as honestly and completely as we know how, then he has accepted us. Because he said he would.

Does holiness sound boring? It isn't. It is the most glorious, dynamic quality we can possible have. Because to be holy is a privilege. A privilege far greater than being a native of a particular country, a freeman of a particular city, or a member of a royal family. For to be holy is to be counted God's. And (putting it the other way round) the Bible warns that 'no one will see the Lord without it.'

GET GROWING!

We know how to keep our bodies healthy. Eat wisely, sleep well, take regular exercise, and get enough relaxation. That's body building.

But what about soul building? How do we get fit and stay fit in our spiritual life? The answer lies in reading God's word, the Bible, and in spending time with him in prayer.

The Bible is a mini library. It contains the precious early accounts of Jesus' life and teaching, death and resurrection. It fills us in on the history of the Jews and the special place they have in God's plan. It contains life giving advice about everyday behaviour. For the Christian, the Bible is the family history . In its pages we can always discover something new about who we are.

The Bible tells us the truth about ourselves; like a mirror, it shows us as we really are, and highlights the changes God needs to make in us. As we take our road through life, the Bible sheds light on our way, giving guidance and direction from God himself. And when we are out of sorts – sorry for ourselves, angry, or indifferent to God then the Bible is like a treasured letter. It reminds us again of God's great love, and gives us a right perspective once more.

If we are Christians, then the Bible should never be far away. We may like to read a little each day, or settle down to study it at some special time in the week. It doesn't really matter when or where you read the Bible or even how long you spend doing it. The important thing is to be open to the voice of God by reading his word. Most people find reading the Bible by themselves quite difficult to keep up. If you are like that, then why not meet regularly with another Christian friend, or with a little group, to read together and help each other?

Even when we are reading the Bible by ourselves, we're not alone. Jesus has promised us that his Holy Spirit will 'lead us into all truth', so there's no need for us to feel isolated and clueless.

How do we set about reading the Bible?

● **Pause for a moment to ask God to make his word clear to you**

Many people use the words from a psalm: 'Open my eyes, so that I may see the wonderful truths in your Law.'

● **Read the verses you have chosen slowly and thoughtfully**

Ask yourself what it meant to the people who wrote it. What does it tell us about God? What does it tell us about ourselves? Is there any example we can follow or warning we should heed today? Is there some practical thing I should do as a result of reading these words? If so, what is it, and when do I plan to act on this prompting?

In the Christian life, learning and living always go together. By Jesus' reckoning, we can't claim that we *know* anything unless we actually *do* it.

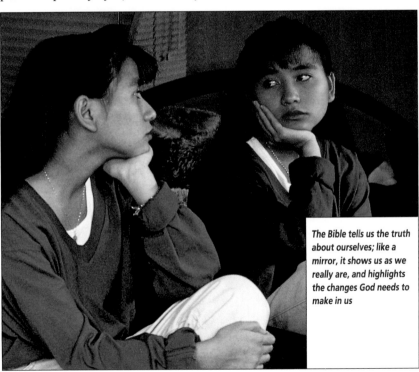

The Bible tells us the truth about ourselves; like a mirror, it shows us as we really are, and highlights the changes God needs to make in us

Reading the Bible is an essential part of the Christian's everyday life. But we need to do more than just read God's word – it needs to be applied!

Jesus said:

Anyone who hears these words of mine and obeys them is like a wise man who built his house on rock. The rain poured down, the rivers overflowed, and the wind blew hard against that house. But it did not fall, because it was built on rock.

But for those who hear the words of Jesus and take not the slightest notice, it is a very different story:

Anyone who hears these words of mine and does not obey them is like a foolish man who built his house on sand. The rain poured down, the rivers overflowed, the wind blew hard against that house, and it fell. And what a terrible fall that was!

MATTHEW'S GOSPEL CHAPTER 7

The greatest thing in the world is to know God. Once we have decided that he is the most important person in our lives, and that we want to grow in our understanding of him and our obedience to his will, then everything else in life falls into place.

If our knowing God depended just on our desire to meet him, then we would stand little chance. Like an audience with the Pope, or an interview with the President, it would be an experience for the favoured few. But God doesn't treat us like that. He *wants* us to get to know him.

When we read the Bible, almighty God is speaking to us! When we pray, we are listening and talking to him! Friend to friend. Face to face. Heart to heart. It's not just knowing about God, it's about knowing him.

Perhaps even more amazing is that God knows us. God knows me. There is never any moment when his love falters or his attention wavers. Despite the fact that God knows the worst about me, and I frequently fail him, he still comes calling. God still wants to be my friend.

SPIRITUAL BREATH

If the Bible is our spiritual food, then prayer is our spiritual breath. Just as fresh air enters our lungs and gives life to our bodies, so Jesus enters our hearts by his Holy Spirit and does his life giving work.

44

Most of us spend our lives chasing from one activity to the next – we're too busy to think, too busy to pray. Stillness and quiet need to be built into our modern way of life; without this we'll struggle to deepen our relationship with God

45

In prayer, we tell Jesus that we love him. We tell him how we are. We bring to him our problems, and the needs of those around.

Prayer isn't just for the spiritual athletes. It isn't restricted to those who are good with ideas or clever with words. It is for everyone. Are you sinful, shy or slow? Then join the club! We can all open the door of our lives and welcome Jesus in.

When you pray, try to find somewhere quiet. It can be very helpful to have a special place where you sit or kneel a place which begins to gather associations with the Lord as time goes by.

Jesus said:

When you pray, go to your room, close the door, and pray to your Father, who is unseen.

MATTHEW'S GOSPEL CHAPTER 6

But even if there's nowhere you can go to be quiet by yourself, you can still make a secret place of prayer in the privacy of your heart.

When you pray, ask the Holy Spirit to help you. It was the Spirit who brought us to new birth in God's family, so don't be afraid to rely on his help when you pray. In his letter to the Romans, Paul wrote:

The Spirit makes you God's children, and by the Spirit's power we cry out to God, 'Father! My Father!' God's Spirit joins himself to

Communion

The apostle Paul gives the New Testament's fullest explanation of this service:

The Lord Jesus, on the night he was betrayed, took bread, and when he had given thanks, he broke it and said 'This is my body, which is for you; do this in remembrance of me.' In the same way, after supper he took the cup, saying, 'This cup is the new covenant in my blood; do this, whenever you drink it, in remembrance of me.' For whenever you eat this bread and drink this cup, you proclaim the Lord's death until he comes.

Christians receive communion as part of regular worship. Like baptism, it is a simple action speaking of what Jesus Christ has done in dying and rising again to bring us to God.

As we see the bread and wine set out, and the bread is broken and the wine poured, we are vividly reminded that Jesus' body was broken and his blood shed when he died for us.

But more happens in the communion service than breaking bread and pouring wine. Each worshipper takes and eats a piece of bread (or a wafer) and sips the wine.

This speaks to us of how much we depend for our spiritual life on Jesus who died and rose for us. We need him for our spirits as much as we need food for our bodies. He nourishes our faith.

Taking holy communion builds our Christian lives as strongly as reading the Bible or praying. It is part of the regular rhythm of our faith.

our spirit to declare that we are God's children.

When you pray, don't feel you have to use lots of words, or spin it out for any particular length of time. Jesus himself said:

Do not use a lot of meaningless words, as the pagans do, who think that God will hear them because their prayers are long.

MATTHEW'S GOSPEL CHAPTER 6

The prayer Jesus taught his disciples was quite short. And he once told a story about a despised tax collector who went to the temple to pray, and could only blurt out, 'God be merciful to me, a sinner!'

But it was quite enough. It was all he needed to say. And it was all God needed to hear.

Of course, there will be times when you find prayer easy, or your needs are great. Then prayer goes deep and time flies. But at other times, when praying is hard, it's best to keep to 'little and often'.

LIVING WORSHIP

Worship is telling God what we think of him.

In hymns and songs, talk and silence, clapping and dancing, we

Come alive

Unless the Holy Spirit gives life to our worship, the church is just another human organization, and church going is just another hobby.

But if we invite the Holy Spirit to fill us with the presence and power of Jesus, we find a fresh delight in the company of other Christians, a new understanding of the Bible, and a remarkable desire to pray. We experience what Jesus described as worship 'in spirit and in truth'.

As God's people, we are called to know him *now*, to be filled with his Spirit *now*, and to let him strengthen and use us *now*. To worship God 'in spirit' means that we allow the Holy Spirit to give lift, power and direction to our praises and prayers. To worship 'in truth' means that what we say to God is of a piece with what we know of him through the Bible (especially in Jesus) and the way we behave in everyday life.

offer our heartfelt praise to the living God. Not only does worship give God first place in our lives, but it does us good as well. Just for once we forget ourselves in thinking about God, or at least we realize how tiny we are in the vastness of his universe.

What kind of worship does God want from us?

He likes us to be honest. Remember that Jesus praised the tax collector

friends and does not spread rumours about his neighbours.

PSALM 15

So it seems that, although we come to God just as we are, worship helps us become just as he is. Worship is a transformer!

Again, worship is a 'together' activity. Of course, we can praise God and pray to him when we are on our own. But there is something vitally important about meeting with others as well. It reminds us that we are the people of God not just travelling the same road, but sharing his life and showing his love. The apostle Peter described Christians as 'living stones' with which God is building a spiritual temple. Paul said that we belong together like limbs and organs in a body every single one of us a vital and indispensable part with Jesus himself as the head.

And worship is work. The other side of praising God is that we set out afresh to serve him in our daily life. We worship God in a particular place, but go out to serve him everywhere. We worship him on a particular day, but go out to give all our time for him. We give some of our money to support the ministers and pay for the running of the church. But even that reminds us that all that we are and all that we have is God's gift to us.

who could only manage his short 'God, be merciful to me a sinner.'

He likes our words and our lives to match up. He hates pretence. One of the psalms asks the question 'Who may worship?', and then goes on to describe the kind of person God longs to see:

A person who obeys God in everything and always does what is right, whose words are true and sincere, and who does not slander others. He does no wrong to his

And what kind of worship does God hate?

In the Old Testament we discover

that God hates prayers and gifts which are half hearted. And he hates worship which is just a front to disguise an unjust society.

The prophet Amos writes:

At every place of worship men sleep on clothing that they have taken from the poor as security for debts. In the temple of their God they drink wine which they have taken from those who owe them money.

Amos tells the pilgrims to Bethel and Gilgal that they can go in for elaborate routines as much as they like, but it will mean nothing to God without the love of their hearts and the obedience of their lives:

Go ahead and bring animals to be sacrificed morning after morning, and bring your tithes every third day. Go ahead and offer your bread in thanksgiving to God, and boast about the extra offerings you bring! This is the kind of thing you love to do.

No doubt they will all enjoy the outing, but it will mean nothing to God because he means nothing to them. We must beware of this ourselves when we find a particular building, or minister, or prayer book, has become more important to us than God himself. We must also bring our lives into line with God's standards. The things we say with our lips we must understand in our minds, believe in our hearts, and live out in our daily behaviour.

Together

Our togetherness is important. Peter described Christians as united and dedicated people with a very special task:

You are the chosen race, the King's priests, the holy nation, God's own people, chosen to proclaim the wonderful acts of God, who called you out of darkness into his own marvellous light.

FROM 1 PETER 2

Task force

Every Christian has a ministry. There is a part for each of us to play in the life of the church and no one else can play our part.

It doesn't matter whether we are young or old, clever or slow, we are each of us indispensable! We are each of us called to serve in some particular way. And what a task force a church is when each member realizes that he or she is a unique full time servant of Jesus Christ. That means that we don't come to church just to be comforted, but to be commissioned!

When the New Testament talks about the different ways of serving

JESUS ON VIEW

God is invisible. He sent his Son, so that we could see what he is like but that was long ago and far away. So how can we know that God is real today? What is the proof that Jesus is alive?

The answer to both these questions is 'Look at the church!' The invisible God, once seen in Jesus, is now seen in his people as they worship him, love one another, and serve the community for his sake.

The same Jesus who walked the shores of Galilee is alive, now and always, in his church. In Paul's words 'we are the body of Christ'. We hand down his story, share the life of his Spirit, and live out his good news.

When we break bread and drink wine together, we remember that his body was broken and his blood shed for us when he died on the cross. As we eat and drink together, we realize that we are part of the life of Jesus in the world today. We are personally involved in his work here and now.

And we discover that our own

Jesus, it doesn't draw a line between the sacred (things we do in church) and the secular (things we do in the wider community). The pastor preparing a sermon isn't more holy than someone cooking a meal. *Every Christian is holy belonging to God, and looking to serve him in everyday life.* The church to which we belong can only be effective if each of us discovers our own ministry. If we don't do that, then the church is lame in our department. If we are lazy, or go missing, the whole church is the poorer.

When it comes to ministry, Jesus is our example. He was never a status seeker. When his followers tried to make him king, or talked of him sitting on his glorious throne, he checked them: 'The Son of Man did not come to be served; he came to serve and to give his life to redeem many people.'

And when his disciples were arguing among themselves as to which of them was the most important, Jesus said:

The kings of the pagans have power over their people, and the rulers are called 'Friends of the People'. But this is not the way it is with you; rather, the greatest one among you must be like the youngest, and the leader must be like the servant.

For Jesus, status was neither here nor there. What mattered was the humble laying down of his life in service to others. If we are his followers today, we must do the same.

Christian group is just one among hundreds and thousands of groups which make up the worldwide church. Across continents and cultures, God is worshipped and served in a splendid variety of languages and styles. The size of such groups varies as well, from the two or three people who meet in a home for study and prayer, to the festival gathering of many congregations in a cathedral or football stadium.

The best churches are those which are rooted in history (in what God has done in the past) but also alive today (responding to God in the present). They are a mixture of the formal and the informal having a shape and structure to what goes on, but allowing room for the unexpected to happen as well. In all this, the right kind of leadership is very important. When a church is well led, the gifts and ministries of all the members are mobilized, the body of Christ in that place is healthy, and the kingdom of God is able to spread.

Some people want to belong to Christ but absolutely detest the church. They admire Jesus and his teaching, but find it very hard to respect his followers!

It's true that the church has many failings. That shouldn't surprise us, because it is made up of sinful people who are often selfish and sometimes stupid. All the same, it is still the group of people that Jesus has called to belong to him and share his work. He loves the church, warts and all, and the Bible describes this odd assortment of people as nothing less than 'the bride of Christ'.

Although it might be very nice to belong to Jesus in splendid isolation, without any involvement with other Christians, the New Testament simply doesn't allow it. The Bible truth is that we belong together like members of a family, limbs and organs in a body, or bricks in a building. The apostle Peter, in his first letters, says that we are nothing less than a new nation:

You are the chose race, the King's priests, the holy nation, God's own people, chosen to proclaim the wonderful acts of God, who called you out of darkness into his own marvellous light.

We can no more belong to Jesus without the church than a soldier can fight without an army. So let's not hesitate to belong to other Christians; love them, learn to serve them, and grow to like them. They have gifts, strengths and insights that we need; and we have a unique contribution of our own to make to them. We belong together to God. And it is together that we make a great team.

We are not called to live isolated Christian lives, but to belong to a family, a team

A FAITH TO SHARE

Jesus never intended that we should keep the good news of God's love to ourselves.

Just as he was sent by his Father, so he sent his disciples:

Jesus said to them: 'As the Father sent me, so I send you'.

JOHN'S GOSPEL CHAPTER 20

For all their fears and failings, he commissioned them as his ambassadors. They had power to represent him completely, wherever they went in the world. He warned them that hard times lay ahead, but promised them that they would have the power of his Holy Spirit.

To this day, every Christian is a witness. That doesn't mean that we are all gifted speakers or courageous evangelists. Far from it. But if we belong to Jesus, our lives are saying something about him all the time.

We may not have passed any Bible exams, but we can still say in a few words what Jesus has done for us. Life has been different since we gave ourselves to him. So if anyone asks us, we can in a gentle way tell our story. It doesn't matter at all if we stumble a bit over the words; the main evidence isn't in our words anyway, but in our changed life.

Meanwhile, God has called some people in his church to be evangelists. They are Christians who are able to share the good news of Jesus in a particularly clear and challenging way. An evangelist can show people where they are quarrelling with God and resisting his love. He can appeal to them to 'turn round' and allow God to make peace with them through the death of Jesus on the cross.

Whether we are everyday witnesses or gifted evangelists, we are powerless without the Holy Spirit of Jesus in our lives. Without the Holy Spirit, we have no good news to share just the guilt of our own emptiness and failure. If this is the case, then let's turn again to Jesus. After all, he *wants* us to be his witnesses and is totally committed our success.

4

WORKING IT OUT

What difference will Jesus make to the everyday
story of my life?

Unless Christianity makes a down-to-earth
difference it is nothing.

OUR NEAREST NEIGHBOURS

The Christian life begins at home. Our parents, brothers, sisters, and children are the nearest neighbours we have! And Jesus said that we should love our neighbours as we love ourselves.

Yet often our home seems the hardest place in which to serve God. It's at home that we're seen in our true colours. It's at home that we are most selfish and inconsiderate. Tempers are frayed, personalities clash, and sometimes people who live under the same roof can refuse to talk to each other for weeks.

So if there is any place where the Christian difference must first be seen, it is surely at home.

It helps to remember that we didn't choose our families. We don't choose our parents, or our children. The only choice made is our partner – and sometimes that relationship turns out to be harder than we thought.

But God cares very much about the happiness and stability of our family life. Our 'standard of loving' at home is more important to God than any Christian service we may tackle for him. What a tragedy it is when one or both parents brush the children aside in order to do their 'church work'.

So many of life's lessons are learnt at home. Children have to learn obedience, and parents have to learn patience and understanding. There are few more ugly sights than an undisciplined child or a self-centred parent. The Bible shows us that even Jesus had to learn to consider and obey his parents.

And the obedience we learn at home will teach us respect for all the authority figures we meet in later life. Christians should be law abiding citizens. When a law or rule is unfair or unreasonable, we may seek to change it but we are not free to ignore it. We first learn this at home, because our family is one of the building blocks which make up our society and our nation. The family is the nation in miniature. If families are sound and healthy, so will the nation be.

It is at home that we learn to love. Because we don't choose our relatives, it means that we sometimes have to *learn* to love people with whom we may have very little in common especially in these days when changing tastes and attitudes can make for a yawning gap between the generations. There's a lot of talk, too, about rights: the rights of parents to have a life of their own, and the rights of children to please themselves. All this is just a clever disguise for selfishness and if we can't learn to put each other first at home, then we won't learn it anywhere.

The happiest homes are where children give respect and obedience, but the parents never seem to have to demand it! Such balance, integrity and health doesn't just

If there is any place where the Christian difference must first be seen, it is in the home

What are the pressures on modern family life?

Modern marriage is an extremely intense affair

A couple can find themselves living far away from their parents and friends, and be thrown almost too much on their own company. However happily married we are, we still need other friends (of both sexes) to 'take us out of ourselves' to share our interests, tackle our problems, or simply make fun of us!

A marriage can get stuck

A couple may have chosen each other for purely selfish reasons, and before long they realize that two selfish people don't make one unselfish marriage. So we have to set about discovering and accepting the actual person we have married a person who may turn out very different from the fantasy, film star figure with whom we were planning to sail off into the sunset. True marriage is about choosing each other afresh at each stage of our married life each wanting the very best for the other.

The arrival of children presents a great challenge

Entirely new demands are put on the parents. A husband may feel squeezed out as the children soak up the mother's attention and leave her exhausted at the end of the day. If a wife is at home, she may feel trapped and frustrated with the cooking and cleaning, resentful of her husband's freedom to be out and about in the happen. It is the result of many years of one anotherness. The unhappy homes are those in which the different members are far too busy 'doing their own thing', giving love no chance to grow. One survey in the United States discovered that middle-class fathers spend, on average, a mere 37.7 seconds each day talking to their young children. Yet the same children will spend fifty four hours per week watching television! Small wonder that they take their values from the television rather than their fathers.

The home is where we learn forgiveness. Of course there are rows and frictions even in a Christian home. But surely they shouldn't last for long. Jesus showed us that pride is pa... ...ic – a barrier between ourselves and others which we should happily demolish. So at home, let's be quick to apologize when we are in the wrong, and eager to forgive when we have been wronged. That way we shall enjoy in our families the kind of love God has for all of us.

The excellent health facilities which most of us enjoy have resulted in us living longer. This means that we have a generation of elderly folk who have a special claim on our care and respect. The sad truth is that many old people feel dreadfully lonely and useless – discarded by a society too busy to spend time with them and too proud to seek their advice. But the

wider world. Here again, the Jesus principle of putting one another first will go a long way in helping us to adjust to our changing situation.

Money can be a terrible worry

We may hope for a particular standard of living for our families, or have particular ambitions for our children. Money worries can result in both parents working, and sometimes this can be a strain. In all this it's important to remember that while money can buy comfort and give a sense of security, it is never a substitute for love. The

vast majority of children would rather have a dad than a television!

Bible tells us that a community which neglects its elders is heading for trouble. The fifth commandment in Exodus chapter 20, is this:

Respect your father and your mother, so that you may live a long time in the land that I am giving you.

In his first letter to Timothy, Paul wrote:

If anyone does not take care of his relatives, especially the members of his own family, he has denied the faith and is worse than an unbeliever.

Family life is a living thing. No stage lasts forever. The one thing we're certain of is change!

Making a home together, the birth of children, bringing up a family, letting them go, and then approaching and experiencing retirement and the death of a partner ... The sequence of events may vary (a partner may die young, or a child may be born before the

One of the keys to a happy family life is being able to adapt to different patterns as time goes by

home is established), but the stages are inevitable. Every time we realize 'things are different now', we need to harness all our love and goodwill and imagination to make the necessary adjustments. If we are unable or unwilling to change in the face of these turning points, then our family life runs into trouble. As Christians we have nothing to fear. In a changing world, God's love for us never changes and his support for us never fails. If we are plunged into some kind of crisis, then we can be sure that God is there. He has allowed it, he is in it with us, and he will use it for our good and for his glory, if we will let him.

Don't you know?

Paul wrote to the Christians at Corinth:

Avoid immorality. Any other sin a person commits does not affect their body; but the one who is guilty of sexual immorality sins against their own body. Don't you know that your body is a temple of the Holy Spirit, who lives in you and was given to you by God? You do not belong to yourselves but to God; he bought you for a price. So use your bodies for God's glory.

1 CORINTHIANS 6

ONE AND ONE MAKES ONE

God made us sexy! We are all aware of our sexual desires and drives, and for many people sex is the most intriguing and demanding aspect of life. You may even have turned to this section first in which case, join the club!

Many people think that Christianity is anti-sex. That's not true (although the church has certainly got itself into a terrible muddle from time to time). But if we look at the Bible's teaching, we find that our sexuality is a gift of God.

God created human beings, making them to be like himself. He created them male and female, blessed them, and said, 'Have many children …'

It was God who made humankind. It was God who made us male and female. This should be enough to dispel any illusion that God created humankind but the devil invented sex!

What's more, when God made us male and female, he created us as *equal* bearers of his image. Men and women are equally created by God, for God, and like God. Different certainly (delightfully and excitingly so), but equal.

When a man and a woman give themselves to each other in sexual intercourse, the Bible says that they 'become one':

A man leaves his father and mother

and is united with his wife, and they become one.

This intimacy of belonging is the most costly and rewarding experience we can possible have. It is the good gift of a good Creator, and we need to be neither ashamed nor afraid.

Yet the fact is that when the Bible talks of sex with such delight, it always refers to sex within marriage. God gave marriage as the safe relationship in which sexual intercourse takes place. Marriage is exclusive – the couple leaving their respective parents and friends and committing themselves to each other in a relationship which is

intensely personal and uniquely private.

But when it comes to sexual intercourse *outside* marriage, the Bible changes its tune. Because marriage is the God given context for sexual intercourse, pre-marital sex is forbidden. Because marriage is the exclusive relationship between a man and a woman, adultery is forbidden.

'You shall not commit adultery' is the one commandment everyone knows and the one we all fail to keep. Even if we don't commit adultery physically, we still fall short of Jesus' teaching about adulterous thoughts.

There is a popular view that sex outside marriage is a natural and wholesome thing. After all, it can still be tender, considerate and sincere. And even if there is no love between the two people involved, that doesn't matter. Sex is just an appetite which needs satisfying. So if you feel like it, do it!

But that is not Christian teaching. The Bible brings us back to what sex is really for. It is for expressing and enriching the relationship between a woman and a man. Intercourse involves and affects us so very deeply, that its casual use is bound to lead to confusion, regret, and guilt. To use another person sexually – committing sex without committed love – desecrates and devalues one of God's precious gifts. We also do damage to ourselves, by resisting God's law and disregarding our conscience. Intercourse is the

What about same sex relationships?

The Bible is very clearly against all homosexual conduct. Sexual relationships between people of the same sex is a confusion of what God created. After all, the Bible assumes that when two people become 'one flesh', it is a man and a woman who are involved.

The Bible teaches that homosexual intercourse is as wrong as adultery. Close friendship between people of the same sex is fine and good. But the sexual expression of that friendship is quite wrong.

Sexual desires and attractions are part of our daily experience, whether we are heterosexual or homosexual. Strange as it may seem, the antidote to wrong relationships is thanksgiving! When we thank God wholeheartedly for the body he has given us including our sexuality, with all its joys, longings and frustrations then we can take a fresh run at sexual self-control.

We can hardly be blamed for the attractions which take us unawares; but we are responsible for the way we behave in these situations. We are not, like the rest of the animal kingdom, led by the nose or driven by instinct. We are human beings, made in the image of God, called to enjoy God's love and to please him in every part of our lives.

deepest kind of body language. It isn't just something we *do*. It is an expression of what we *are*. In his first letter to the Christians at Corinth, Paul wrote:

Avoid immorality. Any other sin a man commits does not affect his body; but the man who is guilty of sexual immorality sins against his own body. Don't you know that your body is the temple of the Holy Spirit, who lives in you and who was given to you by God? You do not belong to yourselves but to God; he bought you for a price. So use your bodies for God's glory.

It's not because Christians are against sex that we argue for sexual restraint before marriage and sexual faithfulness within it. Quite the opposite in fact. Christians value sex very highly indeed. It's supposed to be exhilarating, satisfying and fun. But outside the commitment of marriage lasting companionship, love and self-giving it can be a cheap and disillusioning experience.

There is probably no other area of human behaviour in which the Christian is so clearly at odds with the current social trends.

CHOICES

How can we decide what's right and what's wrong?

In most circumstances the Ten Commandments are clear enough: 'You shall not commit murder', 'You shall not steal', and so on. But if a terrorist threatens your family with a machine gun, aren't you allowed to kill him in self-defence or at least steal his weapon? It all gets very complicated when one commandment seems to cancel out another! And in many everyday matters, people seem to make up their moral values as they go along. It's often said that moral standards are disappearing but really they are multiplying.

When we look at the many laws in the Old Testament, we find that some of them have now been discarded. For example, it is no longer required that a man should marry his brother's widow, or that rapists should marry their victims, although there are laws in the Old Testament which say they should.

And when we look at the laws of a country, we find that they change over the years. In England, for example, it is no longer the custom to hang someone for stealing a loaf of bread, or to fine them for cooking on Christmas Day.

So does that mean that all laws are merely a matter of opinion, and should be constantly changed to keep in line with what the majority think is right?

When it comes to making up our own mind about what's right and what's wrong, we need to look at the motives for a particular action. Telling a lie to avoid paying income tax is very different from telling a lie to save someone's life. Killing a child by accidentally reversing over her is a very different matter from battering her to death in unbridled rage. But even when we learn to look for the motives in ourselves and others, we are still only halfway to knowing what's right.

The key to right behaviour is to put God at the centre of all our actions. If he is the source of all goodness, then the right action in any situation is the one which conforms to his will. Christian behaviour isn't about trying to be good or to do what's right. Rather it is all about putting God at the centre of our moral decisions. In fact the apostle Paul points out that everyone in the world has God's law 'written on their heart'. That's why we all have an instinct about what's right and what's wrong, and each of us experiences the tugs of conscience and the twinges of guilt. But while we all have, as it were, an internal compass which gives us our moral bearings, it is only in the Bible that we find God's law clearly distilled and expressed especially in the Ten Commandments.

But what about Jesus? What did he do?

At first sight, Jesus seems to throw the rule book out of the window! He

As we try to make the right choices in our lives, it is often hard to know which way God wants us to go. Where can we find guidance?

constantly ran into trouble with the religious leaders because he defied the sabbath regulations. He not only 'worked' by healing people on the day of rest, but also allowed his disciples to pick ears of corn (which meant they were technically harvesting, threshing and winnowing on a day when all work was forbidden!). And what about the time he allowed the woman caught in the act of adultery to go free rejecting the law which said she should be stoned?

We find the reasons behind Jesus' behaviour, when we examine his teaching. On one occasion he was asked to summarize God's law, and this is what he said:

'Love the Lord with all your heart, with all your soul, and with all your mind.' This is the greatest and the most important commandment. The second most important

God's laws today

G.K. Chesterton once said that 'when men land on the moon they'll find the Ten Commandments there.' That's true! Wherever we go in time or space, God's standards never change.

But of course, the teaching we have in the Bible was given to a particular people in a particular place and time. There were laws about what to eat and what to wear, about health and hygiene, about crime and punishment, and about worship and sacrifices. Among the most important were rules about how people should treat each other within families and communities and how they should behave towards those who were strangers or foreigners.

Many of these laws make very little sense to us today, especially if we live in a completely different culture. We aren't in the least jealous of another person's donkey though we might well wish we had her car! And what does it mean to 'keep the sabbath holy' when so many people work a five day week, with a complex pattern of shift work and time off?

But we can still glimpse the heart of God in these strange rules and regulations if look for the purpose behind them. God gave his people the Law so that they might enjoy peace of mind, freedom and fulfilment in all they did. All the laws point to the importance of putting

God first, of respecting the lives and possessions of others, of protecting the weak and caring for those in need. These are the principles which stay the same wherever we go and whichever age we live in.

commandment is like it: 'Love your neighbour as you love yourself.'

MATTHEW'S GOSPEL CHAPTER 22

So we see that Jesus placed an emphasis on love. Not 'love God and do as you like' but rather 'love God and do what God likes'. The fact is that all rules and regulations even the Ten Commandments have their limits. When Jesus came, he broke the mould of legalism and opened up a way of life based on obedience to God out of love for him.

So long as we live in this world, the Ten Commandments will continue to be our guide. Because of our human waywardness, we need God's law just as a train needs rails. While most of the commandments deal with outward behaviour, the tenth addresses itself to what goes on inside our heads: 'Do not desire another's slave, cattle, donkey, or anything else!' And Jesus takes up this principle in the Sermon on the Mount: that keeping God's law begins in the mind. 'Do not commit murder?' says Jesus. 'I tell you, don't even be angry. And as for adultery, don't even look!'

During his life on earth, Jesus kept God's law because he was sure of God's love. And he held up the same pattern of loving obedience to his disciples:

If you keep my commandments, you will remain in my love, just as I have kept my Father's commandments and remain in his love.

JOHN'S GOSPEL CHAPTER 15

TAKE YOUR TIME

Time is fascinating.

Every one of us has the same number of hours in the day. Yet for some time flies, while for others it drags. We go to extraordinary lengths to save time, and then wilfully waste it. And too often we miss out on 'today' altogether, because we're hankering after yesterday or longing for tomorrow.

In one of his *Prayers of Life* Michel Quoist smiles sadly at our pressured existence:

All men run after time.
They pass through life running
Hurried, jostled, over burdened,
Frantic
And they never get there.
They haven't time! ...
Lord, you must have made a
*   mistake in your calculations ...*

And yet there isn't a mistake. Time is God's gift to us – a remarkable dimension of his wonderful creation. It is for us to take, use, and enjoy.

If there was a man under pressure, it was Jesus. He had the pressure of popularity as he was besieged by crowds, and the pressure from critics who bombarded him with questions. There was the pressure to choose and train disciples who could continue his work, and the pressure from his own family who wondered what had come over him. There is even one passage in the Gospels

(Mark 3) where we see each of these pressures at work in Jesus' life and all on the same day!

Jesus' answer was to live fully in the present moment. The time to know God is now. The time to serve him is now. 'Now' is real. The past is behind us, the future is uncertain, but we can be absolutely sure of the present.

And so Jesus took each God-given moment. He accepted each God-given interruption. Early in the morning or late at night, he gave his time to God. And in so doing, he found time for others giving them the kind of undivided attention we find so hard to give. He brought the healing and peace of God from heaven to earth and from eternity into time.

How can we 'take our time'?

Plainly we haven't time to do everything we want to do. But there is time for everything *God* wants us to do, if only we seek his will.

This doesn't mean being constantly busy. Far from it. It means from time to time we will be very *un*-busy. We will have something of the rhythm of Jesus – time for God and time for others. We will have something of his openness – not getting uptight when our routine is disturbed or our plans are frustrated. We start to see such events in a new light – here is someone God has given us to care for, or a situation in which he wants us to help.

Instead of being ruled by the

clock, we must take charge of time. Try taking five minutes to be quiet in the presence of God, doing nothing and going nowhere. Call a halt to the mindless stampede of a ridiculously busy day, and be still! Such an exercise shows us two wonderful truths:

- **There is time for everything God wants us to be**

- **There is time for everything God wants us to do**

And suddenly we have all the time in the world!

There is time for everything God wants us to be; there is time for everything God wants us to do. We just have to find time to find out what his will is for our lives

MONEY MONEY MONEY

Lots of people worship money. They love the good things it can buy and the good times it can give. If you have plenty of money you are regarded as successful, and others look up to you. It protects you from hardship, gets you out of trouble, and makes life easier and more enjoyable for yourself and your family.

Yes, money is a god for very many people. But it isn't a true god. It can't buy forgiveness, it doesn't secure eternal life, and it is unable to love!

And yet there is nothing wrong with money. In itself, money is neutral. Our problems begin when we *love* money. The Bible points this out: 'The love of money is a source of all kinds of evil.' (First letter of Timothy, chapter 6)

It's a love that doesn't satisfy. It's a love that doesn't last. And Jesus warned very clearly against spending our lives in its service.

Although Jesus tells us not to set our hearts on money and possessions, he doesn't command us to throw everything away and take to the road as tramps. It was only when he embarked on the life of a travelling teacher that he lived simply, trusting his heavenly Father for his needs, and encouraging his disciples to do the same. As a carpenter in Nazareth, he would have been a well to do member of society in that town, and it seems that he worked to support his mother and family for many years.

Jesus did indeed confront a rich young man on the subject of wealth.

But that was because money was the main obstacle to that particular person becoming his follower. He didn't go round challenging everyone to cash their possessions and follow him though he did warn, 'You cannot serve God and money.'

It is clear that most of Jesus' followers kept their homes and possessions. Zacchaeus promised to give half his wealth away but that still means that he *kept* half! Lazarus and his sisters at Bethany

Do not store up riches for yourselves here on earth, where moths and rust destroy, and robbers break in and steal. Instead, store up riches for yourselves in heaven, where moths and rust cannot destroy, and robbers cannot break in and steal. For your heart will always be where your riches are.

MATTHEW'S GOSPEL CHAPTER 6

obviously owned the kind of home which could offer hospitality to Jesus and his twelve hungry disciples. And Joseph of Arimathea was able to give his tomb.

Everything we are, and everything we have, comes from God. So the way we use our money and share our possessions should be a reflection of God's own love and generosity to all people. God has given us the whole of creation to enjoy, but it is for the *common good*. God's law constantly commends the poor to our care. And Jesus in one of his parables condemns a rich man for his scandalous indifference to the beggar outside his house.

So Christians cannot sit smugly on wealth. Once we have enough for our daily needs, we must look to share our surplus with those who are less fortunate. In his first letter to Timothy, Paul urges those who are rich in possessions to be rich also in good works:

Command those who are rich in the things of this life not to be proud, but to place their hope, not in such an uncertain thing as riches, but in God, who generously gives us everything for our enjoyment. Command them to do good, to be rich in good works, to be generous and ready to share with others.

Let's face the fact that money is a good servant but a poor master. Love of money is never satisfied, and jealousy of other people's possessions rots all our relationships. But how fabulous it is

Why worry?

Jesus said: 'Do not start worrying: "Where will my food come from? or my drink? or my clothes?" (These are the things the pagans are always concerned about.) Your Father in heaven knows that you need all these things. Instead, be concerned above everything else with the Kingdom of God and with what he requires of you, and he will provide you with all these other things.'

MATTHEW'S GOSPEL CHAPTER 6

to know that we are immensely rich in the love of our heavenly Father. We can travel light in this world, knowing that he will always provide enough for our daily needs and enough for us to be generous to others.

Wealth is a problem:

● **Wealth can make us proud**
We parade our fine possessions as though they are proof that we are somehow 'good' – certainly better than those who can't afford such things. And gradually we drop the friends and acquaintances who can't keep up with us. We may even move away to a 'better area'.

● **It's only a short step from being proud of our possessions to actually relying on them**
They show the world how much we are worth. And with money in the

bank we don't have to depend on anyone, and can buy our way out of all kinds of trouble.

Whether we are rich or poor, there is no need for us to be obsessed with money. Our well being and security doesn't lie in that direction at all. Our trust is in a *Person.* That person is the living God.

In fact, there are ways in which wealth makes us poor! It can rob us of the most important relationships in our life. If we are dominated by the love of money, we begin to forget God. If we are obsessed with wealth, we begin to respect some people, and dismiss others, in the light of their possessions. Barriers go up between us and our fellow human beings.

Jesus once declared a principle, and reinforced it with a parable:

Watch out and guard yourselves from every kind of greed; because a

Giving the Jesus way

Jesus said our giving should be secret:

When you help a needy person, do it in such a way that even your closest friend will not know about it. Then it will be a private matter.
MATTHEW'S GOSPEL CHAPTER 6

In his second letter to the Corinthians, Paul said that our giving should be thoughtful, voluntary and cheerful:

Each one should give as he has decided, not with regret or out of a sense of duty; for God loves the one who gives gladly.

And he points out that we simply can't lose!

And God is able to give you more than you need, so that you will always have all you need for yourselves and more than enough for every good cause.

person's true life is not made up of the things he owns, no matter how rich he may be.

There was once a rich man who had land which bore good crops. He began to think to himself, 'I haven't anywhere to keep all my crops. What can I do? This is what I will do,' he told himself; 'I will tear down my barns and build bigger ones, where I will store my corn and all my other goods. Then I will say to myself, Lucky man! You have all the good things you need for many years. Take life easy, eat, drink, and enjoy yourself!'

But God told the man, 'You fool! This very night you will have to give up your life; then who will get all these things you have kept for yourself?'

And Jesus concluded, 'This is how it is with those who pile up riches for themselves but are not rich in God's sight.'

LUKE'S GOSPEL CHAPTER 12

I have learnt to be satisfied with what I have. I know what it is to be in need and what it is to have more than enough. I have learnt this secret, so that anywhere, and anytime, I am content, whether I am full or hungry, whether I have too much or too little. I have the strength to face all conditions by the power that Christ gave me.

PAUL'S LETTER TO THE PHILIPPIANS

WORK: THE FIVE DAY BORE?

We live in a world of work. Most of us spend the best part of each day, and many days in the week, at work. Not only do we depend on work for our livelihood, but our society depends on our work for its survival.

And yet many people resent the everyday routine. Some find their work too pressured and hectic, while others are listless and bored. The working week is something to be endured longing for the weekends and holidays to make it all worthwhile. Work is at best an unfortunate necessity, and at worst a downright nuisance.

But it would be a tragedy if Christians were to view work in this way.

For a start, our work is God given. And all God's gifts are good. The story of creation in Genesis makes it clear that he has given the whole world into our care:

God created human beings, making them to be like himself. He created them male and female, blessed them, and said, 'Have many children, so that your descendants will live all over the earth and bring it under their control.'

God has also made us to belong together in communities. That means that we belong together with our neighbours in an intricate network of giving and receiving, producing and consuming. If this 'one anotherness' is God given, then we can be pleased to be involved in the well being of others, and proud of the part we have to play.

Our everyday work is the main Christian ministry God has given us. Christians don't go to work in search of wealth or status or even security. We go to work because this is the major way God has given us by which we serve the community for his sake. In so doing we help to make up the human society in which God intends us to live. God looks for a society in which men, women and children can enjoy fulfilling lives and grow to maturity in freedom and peace.

So our job is not to be regarded as some form of torture! It is a glad co-operation with God in the whole of his plan for humanity.

But how do I know what God wants me to do?

Work is certainly not divided into bits that God calls people to do, and other bits they take up on their own. All work is a response to God's calling. It's great to be called into medicine, social work, ordained ministry, and so on. It's great also to be called into industry and commerce, government, agriculture, the mass media. Where would we be without those who take on the dirty, dangerous and boring jobs on which every society depends? God calls his people to serve in all these many and varied aspects of life. And there is no higher privilege

Many of the problems people face in life are related to work. Much of the Bible's teaching is closely relevant to the hours we spend earning our living

75

Christ is the real master

Men and women are made in God's image, and the work we do is a partnership with him.

So what goes wrong? Why do people loathe going to work, and why are so many economies strangled by disputes and strikes, bribery and absenteeism?

The cause of the trouble is that we have lost sight of the special value each person has. Instead, we have allowed systems to develop which treat people as little better than anonymous slaves. And something in each of us objects to being exploited in this way. We know instinctively that we are not merely cogs in a machine. We refuse to be dehumanized.

The Bible agrees with us! It emphasizes that people are priceless in God's sight – each one worth more than any amount of money. So those who work are to be treated with respect by those who employ them. And at the same time, those who are employed are to do their work to the best of their ability. So there is to be justice and fair dealing on both sides. In fact, there are no longer two sides when both employer and employee are seeking to serve God.

The Old Testament has stern advice for employers: 'Do not take advantage of anyone or rob him. Do not hold back the wages of someone you have hired, not even for one night.' (Leviticus 19)

In the New Testament, in his letter to the Colossians, Paul gives clear guidelines for both employers and employees or masters and slaves, as it was in those days:

Slaves, obey your human masters in all things, not only when they are watching you because you want to gain their approval; but do it with a sincere heart because of your reverence for the Lord. Whatever you do, work at it with all your heart, as though you were working for the Lord and not for men. Remember that the Lord

Don't look now, but...

Every Christian has a unique mission field – the people at home and work, friends and neighbours. It's good to remember that God has placed us with loving precision among those he wants us to love and serve.

We might not find it all that easy to be positive and cheerful on a Monday morning, and we may find it hard to enter into some of the conversations and jokes that others enjoy. But in it all we have the friendship and help of Jesus himself and that's something that others will watch very closely. They may even expect a higher standard of behaviour of us than they would of themselves. But what a compliment!

will give you as a reward what he has kept for his people. For Christ is the real Master you serve.

And every wrong doer will be repaid for the wrong things he does, because God judges everyone by the same standard.

Masters, be fair and just in the way you treat your slaves. Remember that you too have a Master in heaven.

Christianity is not a leisure-time only activity. We are Christians at work as well as at home or church, and are accountable to God as well as our employers

than to hear his call and respond with whole hearted obedience.

Having said that, my own calling will be clarified in the gifts God has given me, and in the wise advice of others. I am a unique person different from everyone else in my physical make-up, my upbringing and education, personality, temperament, and gifts. I have one life to live, and a loving God who is totally committed to my freedom and fulfilment. I can safely commit my life's work to him, asking for his guidance in the choice I make, his

vision and strength for the work I do, and his clear leading in the event of any change.

But what if there is no work?

Unemployment is a scourge in many countries of the world.

It is a terrible trauma to be given the sack or declared redundant. It is frustrating and demoralizing to pass an exam or complete a training course only to join the dole queue.

When this happens to Christians, we experience the same agony of rejection and worry as everyone else. But at the same time we can be sure that we are not on the scrap heap from God's point of view. He knows all about us, where we are, and what we're going through. And his loving plan for our life doesn't depend on whether or not we have a job!

Most of us will find ourselves unemployed at least once in our lives, and perhaps for a daunting length of time. We certainly have to depend on God in a way that we have never done before! Some Christians have found that this is a chance to pray, take stock, and look around. It can be an opportunity to re-train for some new sphere of work, to move to a different area, or even become self-employed. And again, it's surprising how each day brings openings for quietly helping others – opportunities of serving God which have a satisfaction and reward all their own.

Should a Christian go on strike?

Many trade unions had Christian aims when they were first formed. They were concerned with a fair day's work for a fair day's pay. They wanted to put an end to the injustices of child labour, appallingly low wages, and dangerous conditions. Over the years, they have transformed the lives and welfare of many millions of people.

But the truth is that a trade union's best weapon is the calling of a strike. And that presents the Christian employee with a difficult choice. Does he or she best please God by resisting such action or by going along with it?

The answer will depend on the reasons for the strike and the results it may have. An employee is absolutely free to to withdraw labour if the conditions are intolerable or the pay is unfair. But if the reasons behind a strike are sheer greed or bullying, the Christian will do well to resist it as well as he or she can. Again, in some occupations – those on which our society depends for health and safety – it would seem almost impossible to strike. Every other avenue of negotiation must surely be explored before such drastic action is taken.

At the same time, Christians at work should be in the forefront of all that is positive. There is a crying need for industrialists who will pioneer good labour relations, who will seek to relieve the monotony suffered by their employees, and involve them in decision-making and profit-sharing. There is a need for politicians who will press for new structures in industry and strive to bring in legislation which will foster freedom and justice.

MY VERY GOOD FRIEND TEMPTATION!

Jesus was tempted – *really* tempted. Subjected to far more pressure than we have ever experienced, because we have given in, but he didn't. Paul spoke for all of us when he wrote in his letter to the Romans:

I do not understand what I do; for I don't do what I would like to do, but instead I do what I hate.

When Jesus was tempted by Satan in the wilderness, shortly after his baptism, all the ideas of the enemy seemed good.

Jesus was invited to help himself by turning stones to bread; to promote himself by jumping from the highest point of the temple; or to obtain world power by bowing to the devil and then ruling the world for good. They were all excellent suggestions, and for Jesus the Messiah, at the outset of his ministry, they must have exercised a powerful attraction.

But Jesus countered them, not with the aid of any special inside knowledge, but by reference to his Bible – the same guidance that was available to any other adult Jew. The temptations may have seemed good, but they weren't God's best. Being the Son of God didn't mean a licence to indulge himself with tricks or ensure publicity through sensational stunts. Being the Son of God would be the very opposite of self-centredness. As Jesus put it in the months that followed:

If anyone wants to come with me, he must forget self, take up his cross every day, and follow me. For whoever wants to save his own life will lose it, but whoever loses his life for my sake will save it.

LUKE'S GOSPEL CHAPTER 9

For all of us, temptation is a fact of life. Satan is a most determined enemy who constantly tries to draw us back into his orbit. If he can turn us aside from the path of obedience to God, however slightly, he is well pleased. Once he has achieved that, our old nature is alive and well within us, and able to do the rest. James wrote:

A person is tempted when he is drawn away and trapped by his own evil desire. Then his evil desire conceives and gives birth to sin; and sin, when it is full grown, gives birth to death.

But temptation doesn't have to lead to defeat. It can be the means of attaining spiritual fitness! Martin Luther used to pay tribute to the devil, claiming that Satan's efforts had done so much to refine him!

The truth is that, as Christians, we are under God's protection. He never allows us to be tempted beyond what we can bear. Whatever the situation, there is always an escape route. Every temptation is evidence that we have a God given free will.

The battle against temptation is a battle for the mind. When we

79

5

WIDER STILL AND WIDER

If Jesus is good news at all, he is good news for all.
Not just good news for individuals or good news
for the church, but good news for the world,
good news for the cosmos.

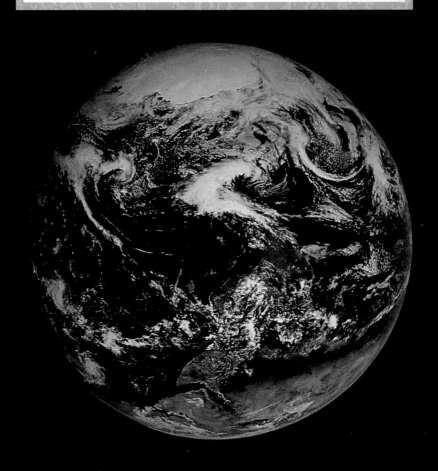

GOD'S KINGDOM

When Jesus preached to the crowds in Galilee, he told them to watch out for the kingdom of God.

'The kingdom is coming,' he said. Indeed, it had already come. Creeping up. Breaking in. Growing secretly like a seed; expanding dramatically like yeast... Whichever way Jesus described the kingdom, there was no mistaking his message.

By 'the kingdom of God', Jesus didn't mean a country or continent with geographical boundaries. God's kingdom isn't a place you can find on any map. Rather the kingdom is wherever God rules. Wherever his love and healing power are taking effect breaking the deadlock of sin, setting people free, and changing the systems and attitudes which dominate our world.

The kingdom is about forgiveness – a forgiveness to be shared and spread. God in his love has forgiven us a colossal debt, and we in turn should forgive others when they have done us wrong.

The kingdom is about humility. We discover the kingdom when we turn to God in childlike trust simply and gladly accepting his love and his rule.

Is the kingdom here? Yes, it is. The 'effect' of God can be seen in the hearts and lives of his people.

But, in another way, the kingdom is still coming. In the Lord's Prayer, we say 'Thy kingdom come', and we look for God's lordship to be accepted and asserted throughout the world.

In the meantime, we discover the kingdom by living the good news. It is the life of the Jesus family. We are part of it, and an example of it. We are a group of people gathered around Jesus but open. Open to love and serve the world he came to save.

And because he loves the world, we too must put its needs high on our agenda. We should be eager to see our world through his eyes; to concern ourselves with the proper care of creation; to challenge cruel regimes, and change unjust situations.

Jesus came to heal and help to rescue the poor, the sick, and the oppressed. If we are his people, we must do the same. And surely the world longs for a church which will catch up with where Jesus is today!

OUR FELLOW PASSENGERS

The planet earth has been described as a spaceship on which there are 4.3 billion passengers. Of these, about a fifth are travelling first class. They live in affluence, consuming four fifths of the world's income. But many of the other passengers aren't so fortunate. In fact eight hundred million of those who travel third and fourth class are destitute. Not only do they lack the basic necessities of life, but ten thousand die every day from exposure, disease, or starvation.

The first class passengers are not entirely heartless. Those who live in the United States, Western Europe, and Japan contribute about thirty billion dollars each year to development projects in the Third World. It may sound a lot, but really it's a paltry sum compared with the six hundred and thirty billion dollars they spend on armaments over the same period.

How long will the followers of Jesus tolerate such a state of affairs? Doesn't God constantly call us to share the earth's resources more evenly, to give aid to the poor, and to champion the causes of those who are powerless?

Where do we start?

We need first of all to steep ourselves in the mind of Jesus. He reached out to the poor. The poor in pocket and the poor in spirit. He didn't just express his concern, or mail them a cheque. He got personally involved with them. He shared their life.

If we are to go the Jesus way, we must realize that we cannot love God and ignore our Third World neighbour. We cannot love God and greedily cling to our wealth. It is *not* a basic human right to have a rise of income each year, a new car every five years, and an expensive annual holiday!

Of course, those who live in

industrialized nations are caught in, and compromised by, consumer societies. Nothing is to be gained by giving all possessions away and 'coming out in sympathy' with the poor. But all of us can start to live more simply, share more readily, and give more generously.

And there is a marvellous blessing to be found in putting ourselves out to meet the needs of others. That blessing is that we discover Jesus himself is on the receiving end of our love.

IN ON THE ACTION

Politics is the art of organizing and governing communities and nations. Unfortunately, because human nature is basically selfish, politics has too often become the happy hunting ground of people who want power for themselves. A career in politics can be a massive ego trip, rather than a life of service to the community.

But it need not be so. The impact of Jesus in the sphere of politics has been, literally, world changing. During his time on earth, he lived and preached in an occupied country, and belonged to a race which was deeply divided politically. Among the Jews, there were the Sadducees who openly collaborated with the Roman government, the Pharisees who hated the Romans and longed for God to intervene, and the Zealots who planned to throw out the Romans by armed revolution. Yet such was the freedom of Jesus, that he was able to challenge each attitude with a better, higher way.

His way was service and suffering. Whether he was speaking to large crowds or talking to small groups, he was clearly on the side of the losers rather than the establishment. His aim was always to make God the Lord of everything – every person and every situation. And he did this by serving people ministering to them. Even today we pay tribute to the Jesus style when

I was hungry and you fed me, thirsty and you gave me a drink; I was a stranger and you received me in your homes, naked and you clothed me; I was sick and you took care of me, in prison and you visited me ... I tell you, whenever you did this for one of the least important of these brothers of mine, you did it for me!

MATTHEW'S GOSPEL CHAPTER 25

85

One person's work

William Wilberforce (1759–1833) did more than any other person to secure the abolition of slavery.

Working as a member of the English Parliament, it took him twenty years to get the trade itself abolished by banning the carrying of slaves like cattle across the Atlantic from Africa to the West Indies and America. After that he spent another twenty-six years securing the release of the slaves themselves.

In all that he did, Wilberforce deliberately set out to make goodness fashionable. Not an easy thing to do but he succeeded. And in

Parliament he built up a team, M.P.s of all parties, who were not only superbly talented, but also completely united in a common commitment to Christ.

It was Wilberforce's belief that if you want to help humanity, you begin by taking notice of

God. He held that when a person submits to Christ, it is the most important *political* decision, as well as a life changing personal decision. For William Wilberforce, Christ was the driving force of both his private and public life.

we speak of government 'ministers' and public 'servants'.

Jesus was determined to fight with God's weapons of love and justice renouncing all other means of achieving his ends. When the Jewish and Roman authorities combined to eliminate him, his disciples deserted him, and the crowd yelled for his execution he went quietly to the cross. For a time it seemed that he had lost everything, that his way of peace and love and freedom was a recipe for failure and humiliation. But

through it all, God raised his Son from death to life and from defeat to victory.

Jesus called his followers 'salt' and 'light'. We are to be like salt in our society improving the flavour of life, promoting all that is good, and hindering all that is bad. We are to be like light in a dark world reflecting the light of God's love in places where there is the darkness of sin and despair.

Would Jesus be a capitalist if he lived on earth today? Surely he would attack the selfishness and greed which is the bane of the capitalist system.

Would he be a Marxist? No doubt he would have agreed with Marx in many of his aims to bring in new social structures.

But Jesus would want to go deeper. Social structures are all very well, and important in shaping people's opinions and habits. But they can't change human nature.

In seeking to build a new society, only Jesus is able to start with the most basic ingredient of all new hearts, new attitudes, within people themselves.

DOWN WITH THE BARRIERS

Today suspicion and hostility between races is still a running sore in many a community.

Sometimes the hostility arises because of the difference in colour between one person and another. A white may see a black as an unwelcome intruder – a threat to a person's way of life, and perhaps a competitor for jobs. Sometimes the racial conflict has its roots in history, as when Arabs and Israelis clash in the Middle East, or when Protestants and Catholics confront one another in Northern Ireland. In such situations, it's not that the colour of skin is different, but that the two sides are bent on defending their

particular religious beliefs and cultural values. Such conflicts are handed down from one generation to another, and are desperately difficult to resolve. After all, who can devise a law which requires enemies to love each other?

But this is where the Christian difference comes in. The Bible teaches clearly that all people are created in God's image. Differences of culture and colour are to be appreciated and enjoyed as part of the wonderful variety of God's world.

For the apostle Peter, his great hang up was the deep divide between Jews and non-Jews. It was only when God spoke to him through a dramatic dream that he realized God loves all people

equally. As a result, he crossed the threshold of a Roman household for the first time in his life, with the words, 'I now realize that it is true that God treats everyone on the same basis. Whoever worships him and does what is right is acceptable to him, no matter what race he belongs to.' (The book of Acts chapter 10)

Paul also saw the death of Jesus doing a demolition job on the barrier between Jews and non-Jews. Jesus had been the peacemaker – the one who brought the two sides together, even though it cost him his life:

For Christ himself has brought us peace by making Jews and Gentiles one people. With his own body he broke down the wall that separated them and kept them enemies.

THE LETTER TO THE EPHESIANS CHAPTER 2

The New Testament leaves us in no doubt that we should enjoy a taste of heaven here on earth by treating men and women of every race as our brothers and sisters. We should welcome strangers, and have a special care for immigrants. The Old Testament law laid great stress on showing love to members of minority groups not just tolerating them, or treating them well, but *loving* them. In other words, God wants us to go beyond commissions for Equal Opportunities, to tackle the bias and prejudice that may be lurking in our hearts. After all, there are no strangers in heaven! The writer of the book of Revelation

describes the scene:

After this I looked, and there was an enormous crowd – no one could count all the people! They were from every race, tribe, nation, and language, and they stood in front of the throne and of the Lamb, dressed in white robes and holding palm branches in their hands. They called out in a loud voice: 'Salvation comes from our God, who sits on the throne, and from the Lamb!'

PARTNERS

One of the greatest inequalities in our world is not between rich and poor, or black and white, but between men and women.

It is only comparatively recently, in most countries, that women have been allowed to vote in government elections, that they have been allowed to proceed to further education, or that they have been paid anything like the same as men when pursuing their chosen career.

But despite these important steps forward, many grievances remain. To those who campaign for women's liberation, the Christian church seems as chauvinist an institution as any on the face of the earth. God is referred to as 'Father', the priesthood male dominated, and the Saviour of the world was a man!

But this is not the whole truth. In the Old Testament, we find the prophet Isaiah describing God as like a young mother, loving and

comforting her children. In the New Testament, we find Jesus having 'compassion' on people in need feeling for them with a depth of love and longing which is more common among women than men. And, taking the Bible as a whole, not only are men and women created equal, but women feature prominently in God's plan. Jesus was far ahead of his time in the way he treated women, in the respect he gave them, and the understanding that he showed.

In one of his letters, Paul included sexism with racism and class distinction as three areas of breakdown that Jesus came to deal with.

The emphasis in the Bible is that men and women are equal but different. Both men and women can work for a living, and both share the responsibility of the upbringing of children. The fact that it is the women who bear the babies makes it more likely that they will be the ones to stay at home, but the Bible has nothing against the woman becoming the wage earner and the man the housekeeper.

But what about Paul's teaching on marriage? Doesn't he tell the wife to submit to her husband?

It's true that he does; but he also urges husbands to put their wives first! He tries to show both husband and wife how Jesus sets the standard for their relationship: the

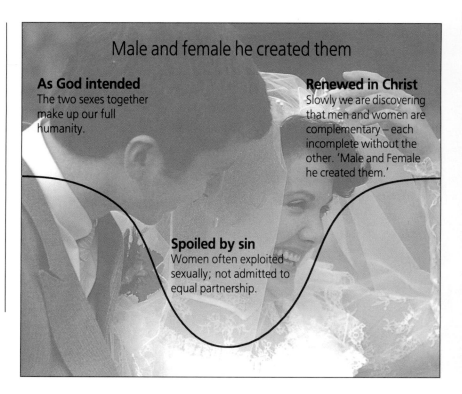

Male and female he created them

As God intended
The two sexes together make up our full humanity.

Renewed in Christ
Slowly we are discovering that men and women are complementary – each incomplete without the other. 'Male and Female he created them.'

Spoiled by sin
Women often exploited sexually; not admitted to equal partnership.

wife submitting to her husband as she would to Jesus, and the husband giving his life for his wife as Jesus gave himself for his people. In his letter to the Ephesians, Paul said,

Submit yourselves to one another because of your reverence for Christ. Wives, submit to your husbands as to the Lord ... Husbands, love your wives just as Christ loved the Church and gave his life for it.

When we take Paul's teaching as a whole, it is hardly a mandate for domineering husbands! His emphasis is on giving, and not getting. He is talking about how husband and wife may give themselves to each other, not who should win in some titanic battle for supremacy.

We read in the Book of Genesis that God said to the first human beings:

Your descendants will live all over the earth and bring it under their control. I am putting you in charge of the fish, the birds, and all the wild animals.

TAKING CARE

We live in a beautiful world. A world of breathtaking variety: snowcapped mountains and stormy seas, lumbering elephants and busy ants... Yet within the whole of creation there is nothing more wonderful than humanity. We explore, invent, observe, love, laugh and cook. We are the 'highest' form of life, with vast potential for good or evil, and the ability to know the difference.

The Bible tells us that we are made in the 'image' of God. That our creative, loving, choosing nature is a reflection of what God is like. He has made us as part of his creation but as the summit of it. He want us to enjoy, develop, and care for the world he has made.

Our mandate to rule the earth and develop its resources has resulted in many exciting enterprises. Thousands of years ago, the discovery of the plough meant that people could grow regular crops, while irrigation meant that those crops could be watered even if the rains failed. Today those same crops have been developed out of all recognition through plant research, their soil is enriched by fertilizers, and their enemies destroyed by insecticides. All this is only one aspect of modern life. In agriculture, industry, and medicine, we rule the world. But our freedom and power have also plunged us into great dangers. Our ransacking of rain forests is threatening the balance of our climate; our headlong expansion of chemical industries is

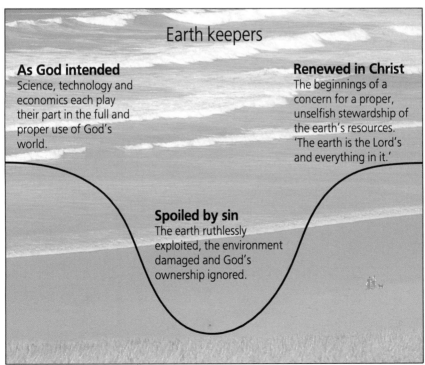

Earth keepers

As God intended
Science, technology and economics each play their part in the full and proper use of God's world.

Renewed in Christ
The beginnings of a concern for a proper, unselfish stewardship of the earth's resources. 'The earth is the Lord's and everything in it.'

Spoiled by sin
The earth ruthlessly exploited, the environment damaged and God's ownership ignored.

pouring pollution in air, water and soil. Far from caring for the wonders of creation, we are squeezing hundreds of species out of existence. And overshadowing all these concerns is the threat of our own extinction.

Over population is another major crisis. Improvements in diet and medicine have resulted in people living longer. Soon there will be as many people alive in the world as have lived in the whole of history so far! But food resources are limited.

The Bible's answer to the problem is neither conflict nor despair. We have God's divine command to manage creation. We have the ability to limit the size of our families, and to share the world's resources of food and fertilizers more evenly. Even today there is enough for everyone, but human greed and selfishness keep the rich well fed and leave the poor destitute.

Of course industrial expansion causes some degree of pollution, and better medicine means that there are more mouths in the world to feed. The good news is that modern technology is well able to provide solutions for these problems. With goodwill, the

economic and political dimensions can be sorted out as well.

But at the heart of the trouble we are in, is human nature. When human beings put themselves in the place of God, the result is chaos. The free for all approach, of wrenching wealth from creation and greedily competing for its benefits, will mean that in the end there is nothing for anyone. We will find ourselves sitting like spoilt children in a desert of

God has given us the responsibility of caring for the natural world and using its resources well. But we need to remember that, as well as being responsible for creation, we are part of it. When it suffers, we suffer

broken toys.

By contrast, the Christian way offers the powerful remedy of a new heart – a heart of love for God, care for his creation, and responsibility for our neighbour. Never mind that our own change of heart is just a drop in the ocean of the world's needs. It is still with ourselves that Jesus Christ chooses to begin!